Understanding Occupational Pension Schemes

Fifth edition

by Maurice Oldfield
Chairman, Pre-Retirement Association
Chairman, Campaign for Equal State Pension Ages
Chairman, Understanding and Communication Ltd

All royalties from this publication have been promised to the Pre-Retirement Association, a charity recognised by the Government as the focus of pre-retirement education.

Tolley Publishing Company Limited
A UNITED NEWSPAPERS PUBLICATION

ISBN 0 85459 878-2

First published 1983
Fifth edition 1994

Published by
Tolley Publishing Company Ltd
Tolley House
2 Addiscombe Road
Croydon
Surrey
CR9 5AF
081 – 686 9141

A catalogue record for this book is available from the British Library

Typeset in Great Britain by
Action Typesetting Limited, Northgate Street, Gloucester

Printed and bound in Great Britain by
Hobbs the Printers, Southampton

Preface

I became a pensions manager over thirty years ago and I remember, even in those relatively simple days, how difficult it was to find anyone who was able to tell me what it was all about. Today, it is many times more complex, and I have responded to the challenge to set out logically, concisely and clearly, answers to the questions I am asked almost daily.

What is a pension scheme? It is an arrangement by which an employing company agrees to establish a trust, outside the employer's control, to provide pensions for employees who retire; income for the families of members who die; and deferred benefits for members who leave.

What is a pension fund? This is the money held by the trustees, not required for the immediate payment of benefits, but which earns income on a tax-free basis meantime.

These are two questions of a fundamental nature. Every pension fund manager, executive, administrator and secretary, is constantly faced with hundreds more and I hope that he or she will be able to refer members to this book with confidence.

Equally I trust that members themselves, particularly those concerned with management committees or who are trustees, will turn to these pages for guidance and reference.

My ambition has been to distil all that I have learned into this book; to present it in a style which will be readable and yet accurate. I should not be shy of revealing a little personality — a few opinions, based on professional judgement. You must judge if I have succeeded.

This is the fifth edition of *Understanding Occupational Pension Schemes* and my aim remains to simplify the growing complexity of pensions matters for trustees, administrators, members and other beneficiaries. Pensions grow more and more complex, and the concerns of the Robert Maxwell pensioners illustrate the increasing need for all concerned to understand the workings of the pensions world.

This fifth edition has been updated to take account of the many changes that have taken place since the fourth edition. It also includes examples of the legal documentation which provides the structure for a pension scheme. My brother, Peter Oldfield, is a lawyer who has helped me with the documentation for a number of schemes where I act as consultant. At the end of the book are samples of the most frequently used documents, which he has prepared. These are set out as illustrations to show what the documents look like; it is not intended that readers should adopt them as precedents for documenting their own schemes.

Maurice Oldfield
April 1994

Glossary

(APL) Association of Pension Lawyers: a body of pension-minded lawyers established to obtain wider appreciation of pensions law.

(AVC) Additional Voluntary Contribution: described at page 47.

Accrued pension: the pension to which a member is currently entitled but payable at *NRD* (as opposed to prospective pension—see below); important in calculating widows' pensions and leavers' entitlements; see page 5.

Actuarial report: the actuary to the pension fund draws up a 'balance sheet' of income and expenditure projected up to the point that the last benefit is payable in respect of every current member. His report, based on agreed assumptions, states whether the position is satisfactory or if any changes must be considered.

Actuary: a person qualified by the Institute of Actuaries or the Faculty of Actuaries in Scotland whose opinion on the state of the pension fund guides the trustees and is required to be stated, and acted upon, in accordance with various Acts of Parliament and Statutory Instruments.

Administrator: the person known to the *PSO* and *OPB* to be responsible for ensuring that the taxation provisions and the contracting-out and preservation conditions are observed.

Appropriate personal pension: a personal pension scheme (or such part of a personal pension scheme) which is contracted-out of *SERPS.*

Commutation: Exchanging part of a pension for a cash sum; see pages 7–8 and 39.

Contracting-out: see page 41.

Contracted-out scheme: An occupational pension scheme which has been given a contracting-out certificate.

(CEP) Contributions equivalent premium: a sum of money paid into the *SERPS* in respect of a member leaving a contracted-out scheme in return for which *SERPS* will take over the liability for the guaranteed minimum pension.

Deferred pension: the benefit to which a member leaving service is entitled at *NRD*.

Defined benefit scheme: see final pay scheme.

Defined contribution scheme: see money purchase scheme.

Discretionary powers: powers vested in the trustees and often delegated to management committees; described more fully at page 22.

Eligibility: qualifications which may be applied before an employee is allowed to become a member of an occupational pension scheme, e.g. age twenty-one or one year's service.

Final pay scheme: a pension scheme in which the member's pension is calculated by reference to the member's earnings at or near *NRD*. Also referred to as a defined benefit scheme.

Final pensionable pay: means pensionable pay at or near retirement in a final pay scheme.

(GMP) Guaranteed minimum pension: the pension which must be provided for a member of a contracted-out scheme which is a final pay scheme. It is roughly equivalent to the amount the member would have earned in *SERPS* had the member not been a member of a contracted-out scheme.

Integration: see page 56.

(LEL) Lower earnings limit: the point at which National Insurance contributions must be paid by and on behalf of an employee and the point at which the rebate of contributions in respect of a contracted-out scheme comes into play (see page 3).

(LPI) Limited price indexation: is the increase in deferred or current pension at the lower of the percentage increase in the Retail Prices Index or 5%.

Member: usually means an employee currently accruing benefits in a pension scheme. In some cases the term refers to pensioners as well.

Money purchase scheme: a pension scheme in which the member's pension is calculated by reference to the accumulation of assets made on behalf of that member. Also referred to as a defined contribution scheme.

(NAPF) National Association of Pension Funds: a body of pension fund managers and advisers, first established in 1922, which seeks to inform

the legislators on the effects of legislation; runs conferences and seminars to inform and educate; and runs an investment protection service for members.

(NRD) Normal retirement date: see page 6. Not to be confused with *State retirement date.*

(OPB) Occupational Pensions Board: set up under the Social Security Act 1973, it is the supervisory body which issues contracting-out certificates and oversees the preservation requirements.

(PMI) Pensions Management Institute: the professional disciplinary body which awards qualifications.

(PSO) Pension Schemes Office: the branch of the Inland Revenue which supervises the approval, for tax purposes, of occupational pension schemes. (Formerly Superannuation Funds Office)

(PRA) Pre-Retirement Association: The national focus of education to prepare employees for their retirement.

(PRAG) Pensions Research Accountants Group: a body of pension-minded accountants established to set accounting standards for pension funds.

Pensionable pay or pensionable earnings: the amount of pay or earnings which is taken into account when assessing contributions to or benefits from a final pay scheme.

Pensionable service: service with a company or organisation which is taken into account when assessing benefits from a final pay scheme.

Personal pension: a money purchase scheme which an employee buys individually from a range of approved providers either as an alternative to an occupational scheme of the employer or because there is no occupational scheme available. A personal pension or part of it may be contracted-out of *SERPS* in which case it is called an appropriate personal pension.

Preservation: the statutory requirement for trustees to award pension (deferred to *NRD*) to members who leave service after two years' membership.

Prospective pension: the pension a member is expected to earn at *NRD* (see also *Accrued pension*); see page 5.

Retained benefits: see page 40.

Section 21 Orders: refer to the up-rating of benefits in line with increases in earnings. Section 21 is to be found in the Social Security Pensions Act 1975.

Section 32 policy: an insurance policy into which a transfer value may be taken by a leaver. Section 32 is to be found in the Finance Act 1981.

(SERPS) State earnings-related pension scheme: see page 4.

(SFRB) State flat rate benefit: see pages 3 and 54–55.

(SRA) State retirement age or date, or State pension age or date: currently age 65 for males and age 60 for females. A White Paper is currently going through Parliament to equalise State retirement ages at 65. This will be implemented between 2010–2020.

State graduated pension scheme: see pages 2 and 54.

Trustees: described in Chapter 3.

(UEL) Upper earnings limit: the point at which the employee ceases to pay further National Insurance contributions and the point at which the rebate on employer's contributions ceases; see page 3.

(WGMP) Widow's guaranteed minimum pension: the benefit equivalent to the GMP for the widow of a contracted-out scheme member of a final pay scheme.

Widow's pension: a pension payable to the survivor of a member. Depending upon the rules, this term may include pensions payable to a widow who became the wife of the member after his retirement *or* to a common-law widow. Widowers' pensions are now almost as commonly found as widows' pensions.

There is a most excellent detailed glossary available in a booklet entitled *Pensions Terminology* issued jointly by The Pensions Management Institute (PMI House, 4–10 Artillery Lane, London E1 7LS, telephone (071) 247 1452) and the Pensions Research Accountants Group, with 53 pages of definitions and over 100 abbreviations.

Foreword to the fifth edition

Programmes of pre-retirement and post-retirement support are primarily concerned with maintaining and improving the quality of the lives of those who are about to or who have moved out of employment. Many issues will be important to us at such times including, for example, the quality of our mental and physical well-being, where to live or how to spend our time. All these and a variety of other factors, however, are crucially affected by our own personal financial position. Having sufficient money in retirement is a central concern of many people throughout their working lives and for most of us from mid-life onwards.

In this context clearly pensions and pension schemes are vital for the majority of people and yet their very complexity tends to deter us from trying to understand, explore and exploit them. We therefore not only fail to take advantage of the opportunities which they offer, but we may well find ourselves unnecessarily disadvantaged just at the time when we are potentially most vulnerable. If this state of affairs reflects the position in which you find yourself, then Maurice Oldfield's book *Understanding Occupational Pension Schemes* holds the key to your problems.

I have known Maurice for nearly twenty years during which time we have both served in a variety of capacities in the Pre-Retirement Association; he is currently Chairman and I am President. His contribution in that context to the increased understanding of all concerned with the importance of finance in retirement and the role and nature of pension schemes, has been immeasurable. He can distil his encyclopaedic professional wisdom and experience into easily understood terms for transmission to the uninitiated with quite remarkable facility.

The pensions' field is constantly and rapidly changing and the details of information current and relevant are extremely ephemeral. *Understanding Occupational Pension Schemes*, first published in 1983, is now in its fifth edition. No other work compares with it in terms of its comprehensive yet concise, expert yet readable, treatment of its subject. This book is clear testament not only to Maurice Oldfield's professional skills and knowledge of pension schemes, but also to his competence and enthusiasm for helping those who wish to help themselves by increasing their information base and understanding of this crucial aspect of their present and/or future lives. I commend it to you and yours without reservation.

Professor David E James, BSc, MEd, FRSH, FRSA

Contents

Contents

Table of Statutes

Table of Statutory Instruments

Table of Cases

Introduction

It is usually better to know where you are before you set off on a journey, albeit into the unknown. In pensions, as you will see, there are a hundred and one variations on a theme. There is not only a better way of doing things but very often only one way if you wish to achieve an entirely satisfactory solution.

In this Introduction I paint with a broad brush to give an overview; probably the last time you will see the wood for the trees, except that as you progress through the book there will be shafts of light through the forest.

The book deals in detail with the position in the United Kingdom only, but there follows a brief glimpse of other countries in which occupational pension schemes are important.

It was a shock to me, literally insulated as I was by the war, to find just about everything I knew and understood was different outside this small island. Pensions are no exception, but there are some basic principles. Those countries which give tax relief on contributions levy tax on the benefits. Where no tax relief is given on the contributions, no tax is levied on the benefit.

It is no accident that self-invested pension funds should have emerged in the UK, with its long history of insurance and capital markets. Although London now has a capitalisation of only some 7% of world stock markets, it can be seen that with Wall Street and Tokyo each having well over 30%, every other Stock Exchange is very small.

Generally, where there is a strong state scheme or state-wide arrangements, private sector schemes have found no room to develop. France and Italy are examples. Public policy which demanded controls on ownership of German industry after both the Great War and the Second World War has led to banks occupying a dominant position in the ownership of companies there with only a small public market. In these conditions, the pension arrangements which have developed are such that contributions not required for immediate benefit payments have been held in the sponsoring company, the book reserve system, with an insurance policy to guarantee the benefits in the event of a company insolvency.

Most countries which would have appeared in the atlas in red in imperialist times have adopted the British system and similar arrangements have emerged in the Netherlands and, to a more limited extent, in Belgium.

The United States and Canada also enjoy funded pension plans. Some would argue that the controlling legislation in North America is even more complex than that devised by those who protect the public in Westminster.

Throughout the chapters of the book, we shall examine regulations of both the benefit and asset sides of pensions in the UK and see how in many cases there are conflicts between these different aspects of planning and provision of benefit.

Added to the problems of taxation and investment is currency fluctuation and/or control. Clearly a Dutch pension fund investing in the US takes a risk that, however good the investment, the income and capital could be diminished if the guilder becomes stronger than the dollar. Exchange control prevents the assets of pension funds in some countries being placed outside the home country, or severely restricts such activities. Many lesser developed countries do not have a convertible currency at all.

As well as currency controls, there are many other governmental constraints on investments. Fortunately, since 1979, there have been virtually none in the UK. Elsewhere there are usually requirements limiting the classes of security which may be selected for pension funds. For example, Canadian pension funds are limited to investing only 10% in non-Canadian securities.

There are special problems for those who work outside their native country, particularly where exchange controls exist, and there has developed a method of dealing with these people, often referred to as executive nomads or third country nationals.

No matter which country or territory is under consideration there are three factors which must be taken into account:

(a) social security contributions, which, however well-intentioned, are a form of taxation;

(b) general direct taxation; and

(c) local custom in relation to employment, increasingly taking into account benefits on death, retirement, incapacity and sickness.

The concept of a total remuneration package has been current in North America for some years, and is now becoming important in the UK and the European Community.

There are many reciprocal arrangements in which social security contributions payable in one territory bestow rights to benefit in another. Pamphlets are available from Department of Social Security offices covering these arrangements as they apply to UK nationals, although it must be remembered that there will be other arrangements applicable to citizens of other countries.

Chapter 1

The rules of the game

1. Introduction

There are well established rules for every human undertaking except presumably anarchy! Those who play cricket or football need to know the rules of the game and even those who just watch find it more enjoyable by knowing exactly what is going on. Pension matters are really no different. The rules are certainly complex but they are worth getting to know because the results are very much more important to you and your family than those of the World Cup or the Olympics.

Have you ever considered that it was probably just not possible for an employee in Victorian times (1837–1901) to put aside any part of his wages or salary to provide an income after retirement from work? Would you be surprised to know that during this time — the heyday of the Industrial Revolution in the United Kingdom — the general expectation of life did not exceed normal working age? So even if your grandfather's grandfather could have afforded to save, he might well not have lived long enough to enjoy those savings.

The three generation family, so common in the countryside, broke down as young people sought work in the newly emerging towns so that by the time they became old, the workhouse was their last refuge. These unappealing places were intended to be the last resort for those without money, home or family.

It seems strange, now that there are whole generations who were born after the creation of the Welfare State following the Second World War (1939–1945), to remember that it is well within living memory, 1908 to be precise, when there were no State pension provisions at all.

2. State pension schemes

(a) The first flat rate pensions

In 1908 Lloyd George introduced his 5/- (25p) a week pension, but this was available only after a means test to show that you really needed the full pension, or any at all, and it could be paid only to men and women over age seventy. Although the means test was dropped soon after the Great War (1914–1918) and the minimum age was lowered to sixty-five, it was not until the National Insurance Act of 1946 that

1

membership of the State pension scheme became a requirement for all employees. From 5 July 1948 everyone over the age of eighteen who was in employment of any sort had to pay national insurance contributions. (As that date was my eighteenth birthday I felt particularly singled out.) Subject to having an average of fifty weekly contributions for each year of employment after 5 July 1948 or eighteenth birthday (if later), a flat rate pension of 26/- (£1.30) a week would be earned, payable to men from age sixty-five and women from age sixty, the first qualifying date for the full pension being 1958. Although national insurance contributions which employees and employers were required to pay became bigger and bigger, it was realised that by the time the arrangements matured in 1958 insufficient funds would have been built up. The State has always operated on what is known as the pay-as-you-go system. To put it simply this means that contributions made by the working population (which were originally collected each Monday) are used immediately to pay benefits to the retired population (pension pay day is still Thursday). Not enough money was being collected to meet the pension benefits which were due to be paid after the ten year run-in period; yet it was felt that there was a limit to the amount of contribution which could be demanded.

(b) The first earnings-related pensions

John Boyd-Carpenter was the unfortunate Minister in 1958 and he introduced, a year later, the first State Graduated Pension Scheme. Under this scheme, from 6 April 1961, further contributions would be levied based on earnings in the band £9−£15 a week and these contributions would earn further benefits above the SFRB (State Flat Rate Benefit). The amounts were 6d (2.5p) a week for each £15 paid by a man and his employer and £18 paid by a woman and her employer. It was considered permissible in those days to allow for the fact that women not only drew the benefit at age sixty, five years earlier than a man, but that the expectation of life for a woman was greater than for a man.

Under these arrangements more money would be collected immediately and, although at a future date higher benefits would also become payable, the day of reckoning was put off. Originally it was possible to 'contract-out' of the whole of the State Graduated Pension Scheme. This meant that if your occupational pension scheme provided benefits equal to the State graduated pension then members would not pay the additional national insurance contributions and nor would the employer. The band of earnings covered by the State Graduated Pension Scheme became wider and wider but the contracted-out schemes were limited to the band £9−£18 a week. The whole question of contracting-out is considered later in greater detail in Chapters 5 and 6.

(c) Revisions of the earnings-related arrangements

By 1968, the whole system was creaking again and there were a number of attempts to introduce completely new arrangements. The Crossman

Scheme was to have come into operation in 1972 but his Bill failed, just days before it would have become an Act, when the Labour government fell in 1970. The Bill providing for the Reserve Scheme of Sir Keith Joseph was enacted in 1973 and set to come into operation in 1975. But the Conservative government fell in 1974 and Barbara Castle repealed most of its provisions, including the Reserve Scheme, and introduced her own arrangements. The Social Security Pensions Act was passed in 1975. The Castle Scheme came into force on 6 April 1978. Although there was a change of government in 1979, it had been agreed by both major political parties that this Scheme would be given a chance. It survived in its original form for ten years only.

(d) The current arrangements

  (i) *Contributions*: The Finance Act 1985 introduced the concept of differing rates of contribution dependent on the employee's earnings. Lower Earnings Limit (LEL) and Upper Earnings Limit (UEL) are, respectively, the floor and ceiling levels below which no contributions are required and above which the employee makes no contributions. Those whose earnings were just below the point at which a higher rate was charged found themselves with an increase in pay but an even greater increase in contributions. The lowest rate of contribution was 5% of earnings and the highest 9%. All that changed so that from 6 April 1990, no contributions were required from employees earning less than the LEL (which was then £46 a week). Thereafter a flat 9% contribution was required from all other employees for earnings between the LEL and UEL and 2% in respect of earnings below the LEL (April 1994, £57 a week). From 6 April 1994 there is a 1% increase in employees' contributions from 9% to 10%.

Employers still pay a contribution dependent on each employees' rate of pay (except that in respect of those earning below the LEL no contributions are payable). From 6 April 1994 there is a 1% reduction in employers' contributions on earnings up to £200 a week and a 0.2% reduction in respect of higher earnings.

Where an employee's earnings exceed the LEL, contributions are as follows (April 1994):

Weekly earnings	*rate of contribution %*
£57 but under £100	3.6
£100 but under £145	5.6
£145 but under £200	7.6
£200 and over	10.2

There is no ceiling at the UEL (£430 per week) for employers' contributions as there is for employees' contributions.

  (ii) *Flat Rate Benefit (SFRB)* is payable to all employees and the self-employed so long as contribution conditions are met. SFRB

is up-rated annually in line with increases in the Retail Prices Index (RPI).

(iii) *Earnings-related Pension Scheme (SERPS)* lasted just ten years in its original form. Although the 1988 changes were announced as coming into force 'only in the next century' the original scheme is altered almost beyond recognition. Full details of these new arrangements are set out in Chapter 7. Those contracted out will earn no SERPS benefit, but pay a lower rate of contribution, 1.8% less than the rates shown in (i) above between LEL and UEL for employees and 3% for employers (April 1994).

(iv) *Special contributions:* Those earning less than the LEL may elect to pay what are known as Class III contributions in order to qualify for benefit. This also applies to those who work outside the UK and who have no earnings on which contributions can be levied. Class III contributions are not related to earnings but are fixed each year. (April 1994, £5.55 a week.)

(v) *Married women's option:* Before May 1977 married women had the option to pay only 'Industrial Injuries' contributions of a few pence a week. Although the option is no longer available, those who were already paying these lower contributions were allowed to continue to pay at a lower rate. These contributions earn no pension, unemployment or sickness benefits; those who opted for this basis did so because they were content to rely on their husbands' contribution records to provide them with a pension from the State. The change to employees Class I contributions of 2% up to the LEL means that women earning less than £74 a week (or £81 a week if contracted-out) pay more than if they had paid the full Class I contribution and earn no benefit.

(vi) *Contribution credits:* The unemployed and those in receipt of sickness benefit receive contribution credits so long as their short-term benefit lasts. After this they may elect to pay Class III contributions. Similar credits are given to those with home responsibilities.

(vii) *The self-employed:* The self-employed are required to pay contributions somewhat similar to those payable by employees and their employers (Class II — £5.65 a week, April 1994, and Class IV — 7.3% on earnings between £6,490 a year and £22,360 a year, April 1994). The self-employed earn virtually no benefits from the State except the SFRB.

3. Occupational pension schemes

(a) Development

The development of the occupational pension scheme has been quite different. The history and style of the business; the profitability of the employing company; the competition to attract and retain employees;

a whole host of accidental factors has produced virtually a completely different scheme for each employing company. There are, however, sufficient similarities to be able to consider the subject in general. The Civil Service arrangements date back to 1834 but they are based on the pay-as-you-go system so that they do not come into the category of a pension fund. The Commission which recommended that pensions should be introduced did so not so much as a form of saving but rather as a means of reducing the possibility that civil servants might make their own rather more colourful provision out of public funds for their old age!

The railway companies, banks, and insurance offices were among the first private sector pension providers. In those days the schemes were nearly always non-contributory for the employee and membership was frequently restricted to senior staff, more often than not being available only to those who were invited to join. It was the tax exemptions granted to self-invested as well as to insured pension funds immediately after the Great War that set the scene for the growth of this sector of the economy. The economic conditions of the late 1920s and early 1930s acted as a brake, however, with the Second World War (1939–1945) holding back any real advance until the late 1940s and early 1950s.

(b) Controls

So what does an occupational pension scheme look like today? Contributions and benefits are subject to the requirements of a special department of the Inland Revenue, the Pension Schemes Office (PSO). It is this authority whose job it is to see that the fund of savings for each pension scheme is only just big enough to meet its commitments. Clearly if contributions, which attract full tax relief, are too high, revenue will be lost to the Exchequer. If it is contracted-out of SERPS, and most members are in such schemes, it is necessary for the fund of savings to be kept up in order to satisfy the requirements of the Occupational Pensions Board (OPB). If contributions are too low the scheme may have insufficient funds to match SERPS.

Broadly, the PSO restricts benefits to one-sixtieth (or 1.66%) of earnings for each year of service, with an absolute limit of two-thirds final earnings, however long the service. This is, of course, in addition to State benefits. The OPB requires benefits to equal at least one-eightieth (or 1.25%) of earnings for each year of contracted-out service in a final pay scheme. The PSO will not allow widows' pensions to exceed an amount equal to two-thirds of the member's prospective pension; the OPB will not allow the widow's pension to be less than half the member's accrued pension at least in respect of contracted-out service. A member's *prospective pension* is the pension he would have expected to earn at normal retirement date based on earnings at the date of his death. A member's *accrued pension* is the amount to which he is entitled based on service up to, and earnings at, the date of his death.

5

Besides this, the actuary to the occupational pension scheme will report every three years and he will compare the value of the fund of savings together with future contributions and investment earnings against the expected benefit outflow. Some pension schemes call for an actuarial report every year and in uncertain times this seems wise.

Fuller details of PSO restrictions are set out in Chapter 5.

(c) Rules

The rules of the pension scheme of which you are a member will normally be set out as a schedule to the Trust Deed. The rules will cover:

(i) *Eligibility* — do all employees become members when they join the company? Do they need to fulfil certain qualifications? Such qualifications might be by age — twenty-one, for example; by length of service — say, one year; by job grading — reaching a certain status, for example; or by earnings — frequently one and a half times the LEL. From April 1988 it has not been possible for membership of an occupational pension scheme to be a condition of employment.

(ii) *Contributions* — are these based on all earnings or is the scheme 'integrated'? Integration means that an allowance is made for the SFRB (State Flat Rate Benefit) by using as pensionable pay in the occupational pension scheme a figure lower than actual pay. It may be that your occupational scheme ignores, for pension purposes, a sum equal to the SFRB or even one and a half times SFRB. This will be for calculating both contributions and benefits. At what rate do members pay (5% of pensionable pay, for example)? Does the employing company pay at a fixed rate or does it guarantee to pay at the rate certified by the actuary as being necessary to meet the liabilities?

(iii) *Normal retirement date (NRD)* — until 17 May 1990 most frequently this was age sixty-five for men and sixty for women. On that date the European Court of Justice ruled that it contravened the Treaty of Rome to use different retirement ages for men and women. The *Barber* v *GRE* case is discussed more fully in Chapter 14. Is it possible to retire earlier or later than 'normal'? If it is, what are the reductions or additions?

(iv) *Pensionable service* — do all years of service count or, for example, only those after age twenty-one? Is there a maximum number of forty years which counts for pension purposes? Do only full years or defined years (6 April – 5 April, for instance) count or do complete months earn one-twelfth of the annual benefit?

(v) *Your pension* — what proportion of pensionable pay will you have earned by normal retirement date? It could be expressed as one-sixtieth of final pensionable pay (averaged over the last three years?) or 1.25% final pay. (Whatever it is you must be able to determine how many years/months will count, what final pensionable pay is and the fraction or percentage to be applied.)

Let us suppose that all service counts and that you joined your company at age thirty. Your service, if normal retirement date is sixty-five, will be thirty-five years. If you earn one-sixtieth of final pensionable pay then you will be in line for thirty-five sixtieths, or 58.3%. If you earn £12,964 but pensionable pay is £2,964 less than your total earnings then you will expect a pension of $^{35}/_{60}$ x 10,000 = £5,833 p.a. = only 45% (however, it must be remembered that with the SFRB, income in retirement will be £8,797 or just over two-thirds final pay). Another question — is your pension subject to any increase after you have retired? It is well understood that Civil Service and most of the former nationalised industry pension schemes do contain provisions which cause the pension in course of payment to be adjusted each year to maintain its purchasing power. In the private sector, however, this was not usually the case except for the guaranteed minimum pension (GMP) which must be paid by a contracted-out pension scheme and which, until 1988, was fully index-linked under SERPS. (After 1988 contracted-out schemes must increase the GMP by the increase in the Retail Prices Index up to 3% per year.) Where there is provision for an annual adjustment, the most commonly used rate is 3% of the balance of the pension (i.e. the pension above GMP). The Social Security Act 1990 requires that, from a date yet to be announced, final pay schemes, adopt what is known as limited price indexation or LPI (which is equal to the percentage increase in the RPI with a ceiling of 5% per annum) for all pensions awarded after that date. In addition, those final pay schemes which reveal a surplus at that date will be required to apply that surplus to extending LPI to pensions already in course of payment before contributions are reduced or other benefit improvements are introduced. This is also discussed in Chapter 14.

(vi) *Benefits on death* — before retirement/after retirement; is there merely a widow's pension? Is there provision for a widower's pension? Must a pension be paid to the legal widow/widower or can some other dependant be selected? Are benefits paid for dependent children? Typically a widow's pension will be expressed as one-half of the member's accrued pension or one-half of the member's prospective pension at normal retirement date. Is there a lump sum benefit and who may be selected as the beneficiary? The PSO restricts a lump sum benefit to four times the member's pay in case of death in service (in addition to a refund of contributions), and generally £1,000 in case of death in retirement.

(vii) *Commutation* — is it possible to exchange part of your pension for cash at retirement? The PSO will allow you to have a cash sum of up to one and a half times final pay in a final pay scheme,

7

provided you have at least twenty years' service. The lump sum is free of tax, whereas pension is taxed as earned income, just like your pay. The rules for money purchase and personal pension schemes provide that one-quarter of the pension may be commuted. Personal pensions are discussed in Chapter 14.

(viii) Leaving service — what will your position be if you change jobs? This is not so much a matter of restrictions but rather what your scheme provides. This is a very important subject; it has been discussed widely in the press and is dealt with in Chapter 9 in some detail. The requirement to increase deferred pensions, from 1 January 1986 in respect of service after 1 January 1985, by the rate of price inflation up to 5% p.a. cumulatively, does not extend to pensions in course of payment, but the Social Security Act 1990 requires that in respect of leavers after 1 January 1991 LPI must be applied to all service.

All these questions are dealt with fully in later chapters. This review is only to set the occupational pension scene.

(d) Trustees

Whilst we are talking of the rules of the game, there are a number of points which affect trustees. Trustees are players, who are featured in Chapter 3, but it is important in this summary to be able to grasp the main issues. There has been much talk since the 1974 White Paper on *Member Representation* about the role of the member in the running of the pension scheme. The National Association of Pension Funds has published a Guide to good practice which deals with:

- *Participation* — which covers the situation where members are elected or selected to take part in the business of management committees or the trustee body itself.
- *Consultation* — the process whereby the employing company seeks the views of members, particularly on possible improvements in the benefit structure.
- *Negotiation* — which is not a trustee role but clearly an activity which may have consequences for the pension arrangements.

By whatever method a trustee has been appointed he has a duty to the trust generally and may not pursue a sectional interest. He must invest monies, not immediately required to pay benefits, to obtain the maximum return consistent with the prudence expected where the future benefits of members, widows and children are at stake.

In April 1984 there was a significant case heard before the Vice Chancellor in the Chancery Division of the High Court, see *National Coal Board* v *National Union of Mineworkers and others* [*1986*] *IRLR 439.* Certain of the trustees of the Mineworkers Pension Fund (those nominated by the National Coal Board — the NCB trustees) asked the court to determine that the actions of the other trustees (those nominated by the National Union of Mineworkers — the NUM trustees) were unlawful. The NUM trustees had refused to agree a new investment plan which included placing money overseas and into industries competitive with coal, particularly oil. Sir Robert Megarry found for the NCB trustees and gave among his reasons for his judgment:

(i) that trustees must exercise their powers in the best interests of all present and future beneficiaries. Best interests would usually mean best financial interests;

(ii) that trustees must put aside their own personal interests, including political interests, however strongly held;

(iii) that trustees must take such care as an ordinary prudent man would take. It was not enough to show he had acted in good faith and with sincerity; and

(iv) that trustees need to diversify the investment portfolio in appropriate circumstances.

The judgment is a very long one and will provide material for articles and comments for years to come.

(e) Administration

There will normally be an administrator, who is held responsible by the PSO and OPB to make sure that the tax requirements on the one hand and the contracting-out and preservation provisions on the other hand are met. He may be the pension fund manager, probably a trustee himself; or the duties may be performed, in the case of a small fund, by a professional person or firm outside the company.

Chapter 2

The players

1. Beneficiaries

(a) Members

Perhaps the principal players in the game are the members of the pension scheme themselves. The National Association of Pension Funds' 1990 survey showed that some 87% of members contribute to their pension scheme. You will, therefore, receive a reminder each week or each month of just what you are putting into your pension scheme. As most schemes have not yet reached full maturity, that is they have not been going long enough for every member to have completed a full period of membership, the expected pension benefits of those still in employment will continue to increase as the years go by.

(b) Deferred pensioners

Those who have been members and have now left the employing company will frequently be entitled to a deferred pension, at the normal retirement date of the scheme, and they too must be considered to have a considerable stake in the fund and therefore be players.

(c) Pensioners

Probably the most evident player is the person who has retired and is drawing a pension from the scheme. The proportion of those drawing pensions to those who are still paying contributions will vary from scheme to scheme and from industry to industry but it is almost sure to be the case that future surveys will show the 1980s to have registered a marked increase in the proportion of those retired to those still working. This will have been brought about, of course, by the very widespread redundancy programmes, where in many cases better arrangements could be made for those with longer service and nearing retirement date than for younger members with shorter service.

(d) Dependants

Less obvious players in the game will be widows, widowers, dependants and dependent children and any other beneficiaries. Except where a lump sum has been paid out and where no further benefits are being paid, each of them will have an interest in the fund and must definitely be considered as a player in the pensions game.

2. Committees

The next group of people we ought to consider are the various management committees, electoral colleges, investment committees and the like. As you will have seen, each occupational pension scheme has its own particular characteristics and it would probably be difficult to find two which were precisely identical. Obviously, the size of the business; whether it is in one location or many locations; whether it covers a series of businesses; whether there are various grades of employee, possibly with traditionally different retirement dates and conditions of employment; whether the industry is capital intensive and employs few people or the reverse; whether the industry is in a declining area of the economy or one of growth; all these factors will shape the type of pension arrangement which has grown up, more than likely in the last twenty or thirty years.

Clearly, if the pension scheme is covering a very simple management organisation, for example, a small workshop employing six tradesmen who carry out a simple process on semi-manufactured goods and pass them on to another company, there needs to be no elaborate pension organisation. It will probably suffice in that instance for there to be a word of mouth communication from the owner, or perhaps a certificate on the notice board each year, confirming that the premiums required under the insurance contract underwriting the pension scheme have been paid and whether or not any changes are contemplated in the coming year. If the arrangement is underwritten by an insurance company, then there will be much less opportunity for members to be involved in the running of the scheme.

The subject of trusteeship is dealt with separately in Chapter 3 and refers further to committees of the trustees.

3. Insured schemes or self-invested

One of the questions I am most often asked, both by members and managements of companies, concerns this question of having an insured scheme or a self-invested arrangement (discussed in more detail in Chapter 10).

In the example which I quoted above where there were only six employees, I do not think that there is much doubt that it would be an insured scheme because there is not a sufficient spread of lives for a self-invested scheme. Besides the number of members, I tend to ask what is the volume of new money which will be available for investment each year. If this is likely to be less than £100,000 then it would be very difficult to spread the money out over a suitable number of investments to give the security which is required by a pension fund.

Provided that there is a sufficient annual inflow of cash to be invested, however, the guarantees which insurance companies provide become less and less relevant and the cost of them affects adversely the investment return which is available on the money invested. This is a subject of very great importance and it is dangerous to generalise. Ultimately, it is a job for a consulting actuary to determine the relative costs of using one medium or another. The only reason for mentioning the subject in a book of this nature is that it is a matter of such widespread interest that it must be mentioned in a general way.

Let us assume now that we have a very complex, perhaps international group covering a number of divisions, each of them operating in different areas of the economy with factories of various sizes throughout the length and breadth of the country, manufacturing all sorts of different products, with production employees, salespeople, office workers and retail staff, even deep sea divers and air crew just to complicate matters still more! There must be a need in such circumstances to have a whole series of pension scheme management committees.

The organisation of them may be geographical or by employing companies or by the different trades of the members. However it is done, the objective will be to break down a very large group into smaller units so that some meaning can be attached to ideas like participation and consultation.

Frequently, such committees will form electoral colleges in order to elect, on a representative basis, the members of other committees and ultimately the trustees themselves. By an electoral college I mean a group of members, who themselves will probably be elected, whose job it is to elect the trustees. In this way the difficult task of requiring everyone in the scheme to vote is avoided without losing the advantages of representation.

The NAPF 1992 Survey showed that 5% of pension schemes are fully insured and that these tend to be the smaller schemes. Generally speaking, it can be taken that the smaller the number of members the more likely the arrangement is to be an insured one.

There is an intermediate stage between being fully insured and totally self-invested, in fact there are several stages. Probably the most easily identified is the insurance company managed fund. The NAPF 1992 Survey shows that 19% of schemes are of this type.

4. Investment

Where the fund is invested directly and does not form part of an insurance company's general fund or managed fund there will frequently be an investment committee. This whole question is dealt with in Chapter 10 in some detail because there are some considerable misunderstandings about the position where the employing company guarantees the benefit levels. If there is an investment committee, its job will be to set out the most general guidelines, leaving the day to day choice of stocks and shares or property to either an in-house or an external investment manager or managers.

5. Trustees

This is such an important subject that a separate chapter is devoted to it, please see Chapter 3.

Chapter 3

The trustees

1. Introduction

Where shall we start? I once attended a seminar, devoted entirely to the subject of trusteeship, where the opening talk was given by a solicitor experienced in trust law who offered the opinion that anyone taking on the task of a trustee willingly could not possibly have any idea what he was taking on. I would agree with that assessment if the newly appointed trustee were to seek no guidance.

I hope this chapter will provide exactly the reassurance which anyone coming to this strange task requires. Since the Maxwell failure there has been a much greater demand for some formal training, see paragraph 2.

To obtain 'tax exempt' status an occupational pension scheme must be set up as a trust, with the assets held quite independently of the sponsoring company or organisation. Therefore, all schemes are constituted as trusts and the trustees' powers and duties are very wide indeed. They are also very flexible, which is at once an advantage and a potential source of problems. The Trustee Act 1925 sets out the major guidelines for the duties and responsibilities of trustees, with the Trustee Investment Act 1961 setting the scene for investments where the Trust Deed itself does not give wider power.

Trusteeship begins by appending your signature to a deed of appointment (if you are to be an individual trustee), or your agreement to being appointed a director (where there is a corporate trustee). For example, many schemes use a corporate trustee, the XYZ Pension Trust Limited, let us say, which company is appointed the trustee of the XYZ Company Limited pension fund. Others appoint a number of individuals as trustees of their fund.

Is there an advantage one way or the other?

- Individual trustees must act unanimously and this has obvious drawbacks — not too much must be made of this, however, as in my experience a vote is rarely found to be necessary in pension matters. Progress is made only by consensus.
- If the trust property — stocks and shares as well as real estate — is registered in the names of individual trustees then, whenever

there is a change in the composition of the trustees, all securities need to be re-registered. This can be overcome by registering securities in the name of a custodian trustee; a company owned by the trustees or a commercial custodian, for example, Midland Bank Executor & Trustee Co Ltd.

- If the trustee is a company the usual Companies Act requirements must be fulfilled — annual meetings, annual returns and so on.

While we are on the subject of types of trustee, it is worth mentioning a trust corporation (as opposed to a corporate trustee). A trust corporation is special in that it must have a paid-up capital of £250,000 and it is capable of giving a good discharge on the sale of a property; a corporate trustee is not. This is really a piece of legal nonsense, but it is the law. Setting up a trust corporation is not too difficult, however; the sponsoring company can simply hold 250,000 shares of £1 and the trust corporation can lend back to the sponsor £249,998 leaving two nominee shareholders each with a £1 share.

2. Training

At the point of becoming a trustee (and I will use this term to apply equally to an individual trustee or a director of a corporate trustee or trust corporation), the appointor should have ensured, and the appointee should have demanded, the appropriate training.

It was as long ago as 1972 that a trusteeship course was established jointly between the Industrial Society and the National Association of Pension Funds (NAPF). It has been one of the outstanding successes in the training area and many hundreds of members have attended these courses. The General Municipal and Boilermakers Union have run courses for shop stewards for some time and the Transport and General Workers Union run a very extensive course for member-elected trustees. *Pensions World*, a monthly journal for pension professionals, has published in booklet form a series of articles on this subject by acknowledged experts in the field. The NAPF has published a series of seven booklets on the subject.

Where it is at all practical, I believe that the most specific training can be given within the company itself. Even where outside courses are used it will be necessary to supplement these with specific reference to the particular scheme. While the greatest virtue of a trustee is to apply common sense, it must be within the framework of trust law. Looked at in simpler form, the duties of a trustee are to apply the provisions of the trust under which he has been appointed. But at once it is not as simple as that, as there is a requirement to be equitable between all beneficiaries and potential beneficiaries (on the benefits side) and (on the assets side) there is a requirement to obtain

15

the maximum return, consistent with safety, on monies not immediately required.

3. Conflicts of interest

We are constantly confronted with irreconcilable differences, particularly as nearly all trustees wear at least two hats. For example, a financial director wearing his company hat will wish to keep company contributions as low as possible, whereas as a trustee he will wish to see benefits at realistic levels with augmentation being possible to assist in difficult cases of early retirement. The position is far more complicated on the investment side. The recent judgment in the Coal Board case crystallised a number of ideas. In that case (already mentioned on page 8) the adversaries were one half of the trustees (those appointed by the Coal Board) against the other half (those appointed by the National Union of Mineworkers). There was no provision for a casting vote. The investment manager recommended that the portfolio should include overseas securities and investments in oil. The NUM trustees objected to investment in industries competitive with coal and investment overseas which they perceived as diminishing manufacturing jobs in the UK. Sir Robert Megarry, in his judgment against the NUM, said that personal beliefs, however sincerely held, must not influence an individual in his capacity as a trustee. Thus in a fund valued at £8 billion it could not be right not to invest in oil which represents such a big proportion of the total value of the total London Stock Market; or not to invest overseas when the London Stock Exchange is valued only at some 7% of world markets in total.

Having established that principle it is, at once, challenged by particular circumstances. For example, if all the members share a common belief, then the trustees can take that belief into account. For example, the Salvation Army pension fund trustees could confidently leave out of their portfolio companies in the drinks sector or companies concerned with armaments. But a trustee of a pension fund of a commercial company, being himself a member of the Salvation Army, would be wrong to insist on such exclusions from that fund.

In a money purchase scheme, the member accepts the risk on the investment return so that, in a way, once the company has paid its contribution, that is an end of the matter. Clearly, therefore, the amount which the company contributes will always be a subject of debate and company appointed trustees may find themselves in a moral difficulty if investments do not perform well in such a scheme.

In a final pay scheme, similar problems arise when there is a sale of part of the business and some of the members are to become members of the purchaser's scheme. The same is true for the trustees of the purchasing company. The vendor will wish to transfer as little of the fund as possible; the purchaser will wish to inherit as much as possible. Member elected trustees will have no difficulty in accepting the principle that a share of the fund (including over-funding) should pass. Company sponsored trustees will argue that over-funding is the result of the company's having paid too high a level of contributions in the past and that the 'surplus' belongs to the company.

Much the same situation arises when a fund is discontinued and the winding-up provisions come into play. The Social Security Act 1990 will override, in certain circumstances, a trust deed which provides less than an escalating benefit to beneficiaries and prospective beneficiaries. This will give rise to the rather odd situation where some beneficiaries (but not all) are better off on winding up than if the company continued in business. To me this appears to breach the principle of equity between members. If all the trustees are nearing or at retirement age they would be advantaged by having a winding up. Younger members would be disadvantaged because further benefits in respect of future years would not be earned.

One of the more obvious conflict areas will be cut down as a result of another feature of the 1990 Act, which limits the amount of self-investment to 5% of the fund. The question of whether, having gone through the process of alienating pension fund monies into a separate trust, the trustees should put part of those monies back into loans to the company or purchases of the company's shares or property, has been with us for many years. On the one hand, some very strong pension funds were started with only an allocation of the sponsoring company's shares. On the other, the clear dangers of assembling all your eggs in one basket are there for all to see.

Personally, I do not have much difficulty with the other perceived conflicts of interest. If the company wishes to sell a property, how will the valuation be made? It is expensive and not necessarily precise to employ two firms of chartered surveyors to try to establish a consensus price. But if it is the company which is taking the investment risk, does it much matter whether the trustees have paid rather more than market value, or if the company is paying rather more than market rent? The answer is YES if the company goes into liquidation but not otherwise. So much of the problem will depend on the company's future status.

These 5% regulations would have caused much difficulty for small family businesses where there would have been no pension fund at all had there been a 5% ruling at the time of establishment. The shares of unquoted companies have, however, no time limit for disposal as it would just not be possible to find buyers. An exception has also been made where all the members are also trustees. Such an exemption will benefit those small self-administered pension schemes where, for example, the only members are the proprietor and his wife.

Another question I am most commonly asked is 'What can I do about conflicts of interest; being paid by the company how would I be able to raise such an issue?' There must be managers who find themselves in very difficult circumstances, although I hope most company managements would respect an officer who sought to keep his company on the straight and narrow path of virtue.

The 1990 Act, to which I have referred a couple of times already, has installed an Ombudsman. Reference can now be made to OPAS, the Occupational Pensions Advisory Service, which, in difficult cases, will refer matters to the Ombudsman. I was concerned about this new appointment in the context of trustees' discretion. If disaffected relatives or dependants had been able to go to the Ombudsman and if he had decided to question the exercise of discretions then there would remain no such thing as absolute discretion and an extremely valuable and flexible instrument would have been lost. Fortunately, this has proved not to be the case and this very valuable facility remains undisturbed.

4. Operations

How does a trustee set about his task? What questions are posed to which the trustee must respond? What questions should the trustee ask and of whom? Normally there will be a channel of information already established but, like so much to do with trusteeship, the fact that a method has been adopted does not make it right, and worse still, the new trustee cannot use the argument that he inherited a system to absolve him from responsibility if it is wrong. So at a very early stage we should take a look at what we have to work with and establish to our own satisfaction that it is good enough. A re-examination of such systems from time to time is also to be commended. But how should we know what is right?

5. Advisers

Normally, there will already be a whole host of advisers in place. The subject is dealt with in detail in Chapter 4, *The professionals*, but we need to discuss one or two of them in more detail in this chapter.

(a) The lawyer

First, the lawyer. Not all lawyers are well versed in trust matters and so the selection will cover this obvious point. Having done that, there may well be non-trust legal points which arise, for example, in connection with real estate. You should not be afraid to ensure that the advice you require is obtained from an expert in the appropriate field. Secondly, while a trustee may not profit from his position as a trustee, that does not preclude a professional man such as a solicitor from being one of the trustees and making proper professional charges for his work on behalf of the trust. Thirdly, do not be afraid, when you feel sufficiently confident, to take routine tasks away and do them yourself. This comment applies to all professionals employed by the trustees. Fourthly, do not be shy about seeking a second opinion nor feel concerned if your solicitor suggests that reference should be made to counsel. There are some very obscure areas which can only be properly researched by a small band of experts.

The lawyer will be in right at the beginning to draw up the interim trust deed, which will be quite a short document in which the parties, usually the employing company and the trustees, will agree to set up a pension fund for some or all of the company's employees. This interim trust deed will contain, of course, the names of the first trustees and will deal with such matters as the appointment and resignation of trustees, who shall hold the funds and other major matters in outline. There will be no attempt in this interim deed to set out in any detail the benefits or contributions or matters of that sort. (Appendix No 1 (page 113) is a typical interim trust deed.) As soon as the interim deed is in place, it will be possible to give members tax relief on their contributions, although full tax approval will not be given until the definitive deed has been prepared and approved by the Pension Schemes Office. Preparing the detailed rules and obtaining PSO approval can take a long time. The interim trust deed will undertake that a definitive trust deed will be produced in one year or two years' time and it is the definitive deed in which one would expect to find the detailed provisions for the running of the fund. Normally, for ease of reference, there will be a set of rules laid out as a schedule to the definitive deed.

There will be occasions on which, due to the complexity of affairs, the definitive trust deed cannot be executed within the time set out and the parties will therefore have to complete a deed of extension of time. Appendix No 2 (page 115) is a draft of such a deed.

There will also be, from time to time, the necessity to complete amending deeds. For example, when the provisions of the scheme are changed or when a new group of employees is to be covered by the fund arrangements, or just to clear up an anomaly which has arisen in the drawing of the first deed.

New trustees can often be appointed only by a further trust deed which will, generally speaking, have to be sealed by the retiring trustees and new trustees as well as the employing company.

Appendix No 3 (page 116) is a typical deed of appointment.

(b) The actuary

Secondly we need to make special reference to the actuary. (Actuarial matters are dealt with generally in Chapter 4.) His advice to the trustees is critical in both the calculation of benefits and the effects of investment policy. His estimates will determine just about everything the trustees do. But it is as well to remember that the trustees bear the ultimate responsibility. Thus it is essential that the bases, the assumptions which the actuary uses, are agreed by the trustees (and usually the sponsoring employer).

It is worth running over the process of the actuarial valuation as this forms the bed-rock of the whole fund. It is fundamental to the proper functioning of the trustees of a final pay scheme.

In a final pay scheme there will be some known factors:

(i)   the names, pay, ages and sex of the members;

(ii) the normal retirement date or dates;

(iii) the dates from which benefits started to accrue; and

(iv) the benefit formula used to determine each member's rights.

There will also be a number of unknown factors:

(v)   the rate at which pay will alter before a benefit becomes payable;

(vi) the numbers of members who will leave or die before NRD;

(vii) the rate at which contributions not required for immediate benefit payment will grow as investments.

Estimates or assumptions must be made in respect of the last three. This will enable the actuary to set the rate of contribution which is required. As the member usually pays a fixed rate of contribution, the balancing figure will be the employer's contribution.

Clearly not all, if any, of the assumptions will prove to be exactly right but fortunately the most important ((v) and (vii)) tend to move along similar paths and it is the difference between the two rates assumed which is the most critical of all figures.

The results of these assumptions are revealed by the valuation and are used to correct any over- or under-funding by reducing or increasing the balancing employer's contribution rate.

This does not prevent the employer deciding to use over-funding as the basis for improving benefits using all or part of the 'surplus'. As we shall see in Chapter 14, sections of the Social Security Act 1990 alter this flexibility in certain circumstances.

In a money purchase scheme the only factor which is not known is the amount of benefit which the member will receive. There is only need to use assumptions to give members an idea of their prospective benefits and to determine the rate at which the capital built up in a member's account should be converted into pension.

A valuation may be carried out for various purposes. The most obvious, in a final pay scheme, is to enable the company contribution to be determined — at least until the next valuation. Perhaps equally important is the need to be able to certify to the OPB, in the case of a contracted-out scheme, that the rate of contribution is sufficient to secure the GMP. More recently there has been a need to establish that a final pay scheme is not over-funded. In this case the actuary is required to use specific assumptions laid down in regulations and the amount of over-funding must be limited to 5%.

(c) Regulatory bodies

It must be borne in mind that the regulating bodies, the Pension Schemes Office (PSO) and the Occupational Pensions Board (OPB) require the actuary to supply them with certification on the state of the fund respectively to make sure contributions are not at too high a level (so that revenue is lost to the Exchequer) and to make sure that contributions are not at too low a level (so that GMPs cannot be met). In each case the assumptions to be made in determining what the certificate says are laid down and cannot be adjusted by the trustees. It is, therefore, essential to make sure that the fund is in good shape and that realistic assumptions are used outside this certification process so that there will be no difficulty with the certificates.

6. Delegation by trustees

There are a number of matters to be decided. How often should the trustees meet? Certainly once a year to approve the accounts. Should the investment performance be considered quarterly? It will depend, in large measure, on how much delegation is to take place. For example, if the exercise of the discretions to deal with benefits on death in service are not delegated, then much more frequent meetings will be necessary. So first let us spend a moment looking at delegation. While, in principle, a trustee cannot delegate ultimate responsibility for the trust's business, it is perfectly in order, provided the best advice is taken, to entrust certain works to other committees, agencies or professionals.

(a) Investment

Probably the most common delegation is that of investing the contributions and other income not required for immediate payment of benefits. This will range from passing all responsibility over to an insurance company, for a small scheme which is totally insured, right through to a large fund which is managed in-house where the delegation is to an employee usually through an investment committee. In a final pay scheme it is the employing company which is actually taking the investment risk and there is a great deal of discussion about the true role of a trustee in such circumstances. In order to avoid these arguments the trust deed can be written so as to require investment decisions to be taken by an asset management company appointed under the deed, effectively giving the trustees no powers of investment in the first place. Subsequent cases have made it likely that such an arrangement would not be satisfactory and that in the event of a dispute the courts could well rule that trustees could not be denied investment responsibility even though the parties to the deed had so agreed. The deed should therefore permit the trustees to delegate investment powers and grant powers of sub-delegation so that outside agencies can be instructed. The real difference is that delegation can be revoked.

To return to a less arcane situation, the trustees will usually appoint an investment committee. Often the composition will reflect the risk-taking role of the employer. Such a committee may also include members who are not themselves trustees. It is also frequently the case that the investment manager will make his quarterly report to this committee rather than to the trustee body itself. It is very unusual and, I believe undesirable, for the full trustee meeting not to have an investment report at least once a year. After all, the trustees' report is bound to contain a comment on the stewardship of the fund and this can hardly be truly a trustees' report unless the trustees receive and approve comment on the investment portfolio.

The trustees must report to the members, and while they will borrow heavily from the investment manager's report they will want to be sure to highlight certain factors. For example, many trustees like to detail the twenty largest holdings and, where property is held, the twenty largest buildings. Most funds will subscribe to a performance measurement service (see page 76), but members will be less interested in technicalities than in knowing how they stand by comparison with other similar funds and against a suitable index. Here there is a considerable need for education, in a gentle way, for members.

This is particularly important, too, to enable employees to compare the relative merits of final pay schemes and money purchase arrangements. I have said, in parenthesis, how disappointing it was that, in spite of the promised advantage of Big Bang and the Financial Services Act, employees were being deluged with offers of personal pensions which just about every pension professional believed were wildly optimistic. Disclosures at the end of the first five years of personal pensions in mid 1993 have shown how justified this concern was.

(b) Discretions

The other major delegation will be to a committee or, in a large company, a series of committees, which will consider the exercise of the trustees' discretions in each case of a death in service. While there are cases which are extremely difficult to decide upon, even the simplest of cases must be properly researched and careful decisions must be made. In essence there is what is known as a 'power plus' trust. The benefits arising on the death of a member, usually a dependant's pension and a lump sum, are at the trustees' disposal. Provided a decision is made within twenty-four months of the member's death and the exercise of the discretion has been absolute, then no tax is payable on the lump sum by the beneficiary. This is so even if the beneficiary selected is the estate of the deceased member but, of course, onward payments will be subject to tax. If the lump sum has not been disposed of within the twenty-four months given by law, then payment must be made to the estate subject to deduction of tax.

The fact that the exercise of the discretion is absolute is an important feature. There must be no question of the trustees (or any committee acting with the delegated authority of the trustees) being directed. If

22

they do accept directions then their discretion is not absolute, it has been 'fettered'. Indication from members about the way they would wish death benefits handled are exceptionally useful but must be carefully drawn. They are sometimes called 'wish' letters (which has led to one of my members referring to 'death wish' letters). Appendix No 4 (page 117) is an example of an expression of wish letter.

(c) Other matters which may be delegated

Other delegations will include more routine matters such as the preparation of accounts, the correspondence with members and beneficiaries, the obtaining of Pension Schemes Office and Occupational Pensions Board approvals, the collection of contributions, the payment of benefits, the safe custody of property title deeds and other investment documents and the collection of rents, and the reclaim of tax upon these receipts.

7. Meetings of trustees

Who attends trustees' meetings? Besides the Secretary, who will frequently also hold some other office in the trust, there may also be invited (usually only for the appropriate part of the business) such people as the investment manager, the actuary and the auditor, so that even where there is not a corporate trustee, meetings follow a similar pattern to normal corporate board meetings.

I have already mentioned the technical requirement for individual trustees to act unanimously but in my experience matters are very rarely put to the vote anyway. Consensus is the name of the game for trustees.

The agenda will be much like that of any meeting:

- apologies for absence
- minutes of last meeting
- matters arising

and then there will be items on:

- membership changes
- benefit payments
- investments

and less frequently:

- accounts of the fund
- changes of trustees
- changes in the trust deed

and for corporate trustees:

- annual report and accounts
- annual general meeting.

8. Membership records

It is clear that the principal objective of a pension fund is to provide for members' retirements, or for their families in the event of their deaths. Membership records are, therefore, fundamental to the trustees' work and any changes must be carefully recorded.

The rather awe inspiring title to legislation requiring information to be given is 'disclosure'. It makes it sound as though the information is given unwillingly. Part of this disclosure is a reconciliation showing membership plus new entrants less leavers, retirements and deaths. Pensioners figures must equally show additions by retirement and deletion by death. Clearly the two sets of figures must reconcile. Some trustees will wish to break down the figures further to show, for example, early retirements, ill-health retirements; leavers by redundancy, own accord, misconduct and so on. It is interesting to note that in the OPB report on leavers, no distinctions were drawn between one leaver and another. I feel that was a pity as it is difficult to ignore the reasons for leaving. This has led to some ridiculous anomalies. GMPs, for example, must be paid even though a member has stolen £1 million from the trustees. The only circumstances where payment need not be made is if the member is found guilty of treason and convicted to ten years or more imprisonment. Not too many members are likely to suffer this indignity.

The subject of information is dealt with separately in Chapter 12.

It may be worth just mentioning here that when a member with less than two years' service leaves and is entitled to a refund of members' contributions, it is the trustees who are liable to pay the 20% tax. Normally the rules allow the trustees to recover the tax from the refund.

9. Transfer values

Probably the biggest headache to the trustees of a final pay scheme is the so-called early leaver. This is a member who leaves the service of the employer before retirement. In the case of nearly every such leaver, the trustees will need to quote a value which can be transferred into another pension scheme. What is to be the basis on which such transfer values are calculated? Suppose a member leaves after ten years' service with a deferred pension entitlement of £1,500 p.a. at normal retirement date. A transfer quotation is sought by that member. The actuary advises that it is £7,000. This means that a cash sum now, invested at current interest rates, would become sufficient to buy £1,500 p.a. at the appropriate future date. The transfer request is not followed up and a year passes. A fresh request is made. Interest rates have gone up and the actuary quotes £6,000. At receiving the new figure the member jumps up and down and demands £7,000 plus one year's interest. He fails to realise that the trustees' obligation is to make available sufficient capital to buy the pension expectation, and that having made an offer at a particular time that figure does not earn interest thereafter, indeed it must be re-calculated based on current interest rates.

Other problems arise out of the Social Security Act 1990 giving greater rights to leavers. The subject of leavers and winding up is dealt with separately in Chapter 9.

10. Evidence of age; date of employment; health

In a final pay scheme, benefits depend on three factors:

(a) length of service;

(b) pensionable pay; and

(c) a pension factor.

So as to determine (a), it is vital to establish the member's age when he or she becomes a member and, of course, to record the date of joining the scheme. The very first point of contact with a member will be when he or she joins the scheme and is asked to provide evidence of age. Everyone alive who was born in this country must have a birth certificate but those who were not born here may have some difficulty. In countries such as the Netherlands and Poland, records of most births pre-dating the last war have been destroyed. Married women will be asked to produce a marriage certificate in order to trace the name across.

There are very often differences of opinion about dates of joining when that date was thirty or forty years ago. Company records may not correspond with pension records particularly where service before the commencement of a scheme is concerned.

The question of age and service are critical in a final pay scheme and the trustees must assure themselves that the records are correct. I have always tried to insist that the company certifies these dates because any errors leading to underfunding will be the responsibility of the company which will end up footing the bill. While we are talking of certification, there may be cases, particularly where the trustees are re-insuring a lump sum benefit, where the insurers may need to know something about the state of health of prospective members. This can range from a certificate that the incoming member was at work on the date of entry right up to a full medical examination where the sum assured is relatively high.

This will not be the only occasion on which the trustees must have reliance on company notifications. Normally contributions are expressed as a percentage of payroll and whereas the member himself is the best auditor to make sure that the right contribution has been deducted form his pay, the trustees will not normally have access to the payroll to be able to check that the correct contribution has been paid over to them. It is perfectly easy to arrange for the company's auditors to give an appropriate certificate. It is in the interests of the company and the trustees that this should be done.

Now let us consider a collection of matters which are the concern of trustees and may well find a way onto the agendas of many trustee bodies.

11. Benefit statements

A member is entitled, once a year, to be given information about his prospective benefits. Most trustees will issue statements each year in order to comply. These contain all the vital pieces of information and help to reveal differences at the beginning of a member's service rather than at the end. Appendix No 5a (page 118) is an example of a benefit statement for a final pay scheme, and Appendix 5b (page 119) shows a benefit statement in a money purchase scheme.

12. Certificates of survival

When we do reach the end of service, which is also the beginning of pension in many cases, we are faced with the need for different certification. The auditors will want to be sure that we do not fail to register a death. Some ask for certificates of survival or something with a similarly euphemistic title. I have argued that for the majority a personal bank account is good enough testimony that the pensioner lives. Where there is a joint account or where a cheque is still sent I make sure that the persons concerned are seen at a Christmas party or a pensioners get-together and failing that, then a call is made to ensure that everything is well.

13. Benefit counsellors

Many large companies are fortunate enough to have a network of retired people trained as voluntary visitors and friends. Benefit counsellors, Christmas hampers and a regular subscription to *Saga* magazine can transform a pension fund into something more than a monthly transfer of funds to bank accounts. It makes the trustees carers as well as providers.

One of the most delicate tasks for benefit counsellors is visiting the dependants and relatives of members or pensioners who have recently died. Besides taking the condolences of the trustees, they begin to piece together the family circumstances which will be required knowledge before decisions are taken on the exercise of discretions.

14. Comparisons with personal pensions

Legislation lays down, for the purposes of establishing whether a final pay scheme is over-funded, that a real rate of return of around 1.5% must be used and interest rates of 9% have to be assumed. Even then, most trustees will quote prospective pensions based only on current pay. Typically, therefore, an employee with ten years' prospective service each year earning $\frac{1}{60}$ of final pay where that employee is earning, say,

£12,000 p.a. at date of leaving will receive a benefit statement showing an anticipated pension of £2,000 p.a. (for a scheme which makes no allowance for State pensions). By contrast, a personal pension provider's representative will predict a pension of about twice as much, based on an interest rate of 12% p.a., an annual salary increase of 10% and a contribution of 15%. As salary, on that basis, would have risen to over £28,000, the final pay scheme would actually be producing something over £4,700 p.a.

15. SSAP 24 (Statement of Standard Accounting Practice No 24)

The annual accounts, particularly the inter-face with the sponsoring employer's accounts, have from 1989 been affected by SSAP 24.

From the trustees' point of view the accounting standard will lead to less flexibility in determining the contribution rate for the company. This may be a good thing for members, in that over-funding will tend to be allowed to run down more slowly (rather than be taken out as cash and made subject to the 40% penal rate of tax in the company's accounts) but conversely where there is under-funding there will be no need for the situation to be rectified more quickly.

16. Take-overs

Company or business take-overs can be the most difficult situations of all for trustees. This is because of the potential conflicts of interest which arise from the multiplicity of hats which trustees wear. Acting as a trustee there must be no doubt that you are wearing only a trustee's hat. Whenever I have been faced with the situation where, for example, my employer was buying part of another employer's business and there was argument about the value of assets to be transferred, I explained to my company's negotiators that the trustees could not be asked to accept £8 million in assets and £10 million in liabilities. If it suits the deal that this should happen then the company must understand that it will have to pay the trustees the shortfall of £2 million. In that way the negotiator has to decide if the deal is still worth making. He cannot rely on the trustees to make a deal work.

17. A Pensions Act?

Some years ago there were calls through the Wilson Committee and rather later than that in Professor Gower's discussion paper for there to be a Pensions Act to replace the provisions of the Trustee Acts in respect of pension funds. This suggestion is, generally speaking, made on the grounds that the Trustee Acts were designed to deal with family trusts and not for the very large pension funds which have emerged in the last few years. I have been bound to say however, and I am certainly not alone, that we should be very careful before we change a system that has worked very well. I have pointed out, on many occasions, that in the seventy years during which the National Association of Pension Funds has been in existence, there has not been a single case of a failure of a pension fund through financial mismanagement, whereas one hears every day of companies going into liquidation. There have been some very remarkable cases of insurance companies crashing; there was the fringe banking crisis where a large number of such companies failed in 1974. Over the years many professional firms, for example, lawyers or stock brokers, have been required to cease practising or trading by their ruling bodies.

The great trouble with regulations is that they offer to the unscrupulous operator merely a framework of rules within which it is fair game to work. There is no reason to suppose that all pension fund managers and investment managers are angels and the fact that there had been no scandals or failures was more likely due to the fact that there was already a satisfactory network of checks and balances.

Then came Maxwell, a case which shocked everyone. Although it was not, specifically, a pension crime, the Pension Law Review Committee was set up under Professor Goode to examine the case and required that the question of trusteeship be examined once more. The Report of the Committee which was made public late in 1993 is discussed in Chapter 13. Suffice to say here that it recommended retaining trusteeship.

18. Member representation

Even before the 1974 White Paper on employee participation in the running of their pension schemes, there was widespread participation in pension schemes which were established between the two World Wars. I have a copy of a typical trust deed dated 1928 in which it is quite clear that there was a management committee of ten; five of whom were appointed by the company and five by the members.

This participation by members introduces a very important dimension into the running of affairs. I know that many members of committees of management and even trustees regard their duties as being vague and difficult to grasp but, from the point of view of the pension fund manager, it is this very lack of precise definition which persuades him to make very special efforts to be clear in his thinking, clear in his presentation of facts and clear of the shortcuts which might lead to awkward but quite proper questions being asked. The risk of financial mismanagement in these circumstances is considerably reduced. I do not think there is any other business enterprise which has so many checks and balances.

It may be helpful to consider how members can take part in the election or selection of trustees. In a small enterprise it is probably not too difficult to find one or two employees who are interested in the subject and are willing to serve. In a larger undertaking it is more difficult. That is why the two-tier system is popular. Each plant or workplace has a management committee comprising some members appointed by the company and some elected by members. These elected members then form an electoral college to elect some of the trustees. Generally nominations must come from those with a service qualification and there will be a term of, say, three years after which re-election must be sought. There may be a required period during which a member twice elected has to stand down.

19. Alternates

It is quite likely that provision will be made for trustees and members of the management committees to have 'alternates', who are empowered to attend meetings when the trustee or committee member is unable to attend. There may also be rather elaborate arrangements to ensure that a quorum for a meeting must include not only a minimum number of members of the committee or trustee body but a minimum number of those appointed by the employing company and those elected by the members. It is not unusual to find however, that where the employing company guarantees the benefit levels, the chairman, who will be a company appointee, will have a casting vote.

It is undoubtedly a fact that one of the most difficult objectives to achieve is communication between those members of committees and trustees elected by the members and the members themselves. I believe that this is the most important aspect of member participation and that as much as possible must be done to enable the member-elected management committee member or trustee to do his job properly. I am not especially hopeful that the sophisticated information which is now required to be given to beneficiaries under Regulations of the Social Security Act 1985 will help members to understand their schemes.

20. Independent trustees

Since the revelations about losses from the Maxwell funds there has been much criticism of trusteeship as the vehicle for the administration of pension funds. Personally, I do not think that losses of that nature have anything to do with trusteeship. Nevertheless, the call for there to be an independent trustee (being neither a sponsor nominee nor a member appointee) has much merit. There is already a requirement for such an appointment in what are known as small self-administered schemes (where the members may be the trustees and the board of the company as well). The 'pensioneer' trustee, as the post is called, must be independent and has certain powers to ensure that the Pension Schemes Office rules are not infringed.

There is also a requirement for an independent trustee to be appointed in the case of insolvency to ensure equity between pension beneficiaries and creditors. An independent trustee could be a requirement for all funds and such a person could be invested with similar sanctions enforceable through the tax approval system. The Goode Committee, somewhat surprisingly, did not make any recommendations except that there should be member-elected trustees who might choose to bring in an independent. There would be a problem, in the short term, finding the considerable number of suitable candidates, training them and making practical arrangements for them to be paid.

21. Negotiation of benefits

One matter that does not fall to be dealt with by the trustees is consideration of benefit levels or improvements or other rearrangements of the scheme. Such matters will have an important bearing and the views of the trustees may be sought but they do not have any sort of negotiating role.

Chapter 4

The professionals

1. Supervisory bodies

(a) The Pension Schemes Office (PSO)

(b) The Occupational Pensions Board (OPB)

These are both dealt with in Chapter 5.

(c) The Registrar of Companies

There are many other constraints on the administrator besides the purely technical matters relating to the PSO and the OPB. In the first place, many occupational pension schemes, for convenience, are set up with a company as trustee and that being the case, all the appropriate returns have to be made to the Registrar of Companies. This includes an annual return, a register of directors and company secretary and all the other returns which stem from holding an Annual General Meeting.

(d) The Registrar of Friendly Societies

A small number of schemes will be approved by the Registrar of Friendly Societies and the appropriate returns will need to be made to him.

2. Pension scheme management

In the larger self-administered schemes, there will be many more activities than purely ensuring that PSO and OPB requirements are met. There will probably be a pension fund executive or a pension fund secretary who will have overall control of the arrangements, acting on behalf of the trustees, on behalf of the company and on behalf of the members and other beneficiaries. The job will be to co-ordinate all the other professionals and all the advisers so that the players, described in Chapter 2, can know exactly where they are playing, on which side they are playing, and the consequences of winning, drawing or losing their match.

It is not easy to explain why pension fund managers have been able to offer unbiased advice to the various parties who seek such information from them. The most likely reason is that the job crosses so many professional disciplines and that it is so much tied up with people that it would actually be very difficult to pursue a sectional interest.

3. Independent advisers

(a) The actuary

Now let us move on to some outside advisers. We have already mentioned the actuary who will be involved right from the beginning in working out the possible costs of setting up any particular defined benefit or final pay type of scheme. (Although much of what follows is based on a self-administered scheme, each insurance company will employ an actuary to calculate the premiums which they will charge for any particular benefit level.) The actuary will need to know who will be eligible to be a member, each prospective member's age and length of service which is to count for pensionable purposes, the member's sex (whatever laws are passed about sex discrimination, it will remain a fact that the expectation of life for women is greater than that for men), the proposed benefit structure and the contribution which each member will be asked to make. The actuary will also need to make some assumptions which will be agreed by the sponsoring company and the trustees. The two most important assumptions will be the rate at which members' earnings are likely to increase year by year, and the amount of income and capital gain which the investments might produce. In addition, there will need to be some assumptions about which members will not survive to retirement date but in this case, there are mortality tables which, provided there is a big enough spread of lives in the scheme, can be relied upon with some accuracy. It has become increasingly important to make some assumptions about the number of members who will not remain in service until retirement date. This is an issue which is tackled in some detail in Chapter 9.

With all this information, the actuary is able to draw up an actuarial balance sheet. In a final pay scheme this will reveal the likely contribution which the company will have to put in to balance the books. Once the fund has been established, the actuary will carry out a valuation every three years, and it may be necessary for the company contribution to be increased or decreased to keep the fund in balance. In a final pay scheme which is guaranteed by the employer, there cannot arise an actuarial surplus or an actuarial deficit. It may well be that in certain cases, where otherwise the employing company could reduce its contribution, it will agree to improve the benefit structure, but that is a different matter.

There are a few schemes where the employing company, as well as the members, makes a fixed contribution (these are known as defined contribution schemes or money purchase schemes). In these cases the emerging benefit will be higher or lower than originally expected, thus using up the surplus or eliminating the deficit. It is still necessary to have an actuarial valuation in a defined contribution scheme in order to share rateably, among the members, capital gains. Equally, members will have to share rateably any falls which may be experienced.

The actuary will also draw up tables to show the amounts by which a pension will be reduced for members who retire early or increased for members who retire late. There may also be ill-health retirement tables. Then there will be a set of tables to show the amount of pension which must be given up in exchange for cash at any particular age at which the member retires. Another very important table, in a final pay scheme, will show the amount required at any particular age to increase the scale pension. This will be used particularly where there is a redundancy programme designed to enable those nearest retirement to retire early, using any redundancy money to increase their scale pension.

The Social Security Act 1990 restricts the normal operation of a final pay scheme by not allowing the contribution rate to be changed in certain circumstances. The matter is fully discussed in Chapter 14. Accounting Standard SAAP 24 (see page 27) also has a bearing on contribution rates.

The actuary will also be asked to value a pension fund at the time of a take-over or merger, particularly where only part of the business is being sold. The reason for this is that members in the fund of the employer selling the business and members in the fund of the employer buying the business will want to be assured that their own position is not prejudiced by the transaction. This subject is covered in greater detail in Chapter 3.

(b) The lawyer

Another professional who will feature from time to time in the affairs of the self-administered pension fund is the lawyer. He will have very specific trust duties which are outlined in Chapter 3.

There are other areas in which a lawyer will be used. For example, conveyancing of property where this forms part of the investments of the fund. Not only are there deeds to be drawn upon sale and purchase, but there will be numerous changes of tenancy where assignments will be required. There may even be a need to send the odd solicitor's letter to a tenant who is not sufficiently prompt in paying the rent!

There may also be a need, rarely, one hopes, to defend the trustees in a legal action, or to pursue someone through the courts on behalf of the trustees.

(c) The banker

The fund's banker may play a significant role, particularly where a larger number of pensioners and other beneficiaries are paid direct by the scheme. Making sure that their money reaches them each month will be regarded by the pension fund manager as his absolute number one priority. Whereas most people will be paid direct through a bank account, there are still those, particularly in the upper pension ages, who prefer to receive cash. Your banker will be able to arrange for this to be done through a local branch of the bank and this will avoid the very expensive transmission of cash by registered letter or in the form of a money or postal order.

When very high interest rates are being experienced, it is extremely important that no cash balances should be lying about earning no interest. By careful co-operation with the bank, it will be possible to place all money not required for immediate payment of benefits or purchase of investments with the bank itself or with a local authority so that interest is earned on all balances at all times.

The transmission of cash to purchase investments or properties and the paying-in of receipts from whatever source they come, must be accomplished with no loss of time and here again the co-operation of the bank is essential.

In fact, cash management is now coming to be regarded as an essential part of fund management generally. Money spent on employing a specialist can be recovered many times over.

(d) The auditor

I was uncertain whether to place the fund auditors under the heading of professionals or players. The role of a company's auditor, besides approving the accounting entries, is to enable the shareholders to see how the business is faring. The position of a pension fund auditor is even more important to the members and the employing companies because the accounting base is the foundation on which the actuary will perform his task. The trustees will also be looking to the company's auditors to establish that the right amount of contribution is being paid over to them. It is also frequently argued that whereas a company shareholder should be in a position to check that he has received the right dividends, many company pensioners are less able to be sure that they have received the right amount of pension and that the correct tax deduction has been made.

(e) The investment managers and advisers

The next group of professionals are those dealing with the investments of the fund. This is however, so intertwined with investment itself that the subject is dealt with in Chapter 10.

(f) The medical advisers

There is one other professional group with whom the trustees may have a relationship. That is the medical profession. The trust deed may leave certain decisions regarding ill-health retirement to the trustees, who will seek medical advice in appropriate cases. There may also be a fairly close relationship with permanent health insurance schemes or accident and disability schemes where medical opinion will form an important part in determining the benefit structures. Although such schemes cannot form part of the pension fund, it usually falls to the pensions office to deal with such matters.

(g) Consultants

There will also be a range of services available to the smaller funds who do not have their own managements. These services will be provided by insurance brokers and pension advisers or pension consultants. More and more these services are rewarded by fees rather than commissions arising under insurance policies. These services may also be used for specialist jobs, for example, a large UK company may have a very small overseas operation and the pension arrangements for the foreign subsidiary may well be in the hands of a pension consultant, either in the UK or in the overseas territory concerned.

The NAPF year book lists all its members who are advisers. The Society of Pension Consultants is a trade association of pension advisers, as the name suggests, and it too has its year book. Then there is a publication called Pension Funds and their Advisers.

The Financial Services Act sought to lay down standards for such advisers. In the event that authorising bodies have established costly bureaucracies and some of the protections are arguably less strong than clients might expect.

(h) The independent trustee

In the light of the Maxwell pension fund problems I have added a further paragraph on page 28 in Chapter 3. Such a person would not be an employee of the sponsoring company or responsible to that organisation. Regulations could make such trustees answerable to the OPB and PSO approval would be withheld until such a person was appointed but such a requirement is unlikely following the absence of such a recommendation in the Goode Report.

4. Who pays?

There then arises the question of who pays these professionals.

There are two rather different considerations. In the purchase and sale of Stock Exchange securities or properties there are certain costs, like stockbrokers' commissions, stamp duty and professional fees, which really form part and parcel of the cost of the investment. In the majority of funds, these costs will be added to the purchase price or subtracted from the sale proceeds; to do otherwise would distort the whole basis of dealing. These costs, therefore, are usually capitalised and become charges on the pension fund itself. The pension fund will also probably bear the cost of bank charges in connection with money movements or pension payments.

At the other end of the scale, there will be as many cases where it is the employing company who pays for administrative expenses, for example, the salaries and other costs of employing the pensions administration staff and the fees payable to auditors or actuaries.

In a final pay scheme, and these form the majority, the company pays the balance of the contributions required. In such cases it hardly matters whether the contribution is somewhat higher, allowing the trustees to pay their own way, or somewhat lower because the company meets administrative expenses. There are advantages in the trustees having resources to pay, for example, the travel costs of trustees elected by members. On the other hand the VAT position is most unsatisfactory in that pension funds are 'exempt' which, rather oddly, means they are liable to pay VAT but they have no set-offs. I really believe it was intended that funds should have been 'zero-rated', but some ten years of negotiation by the NAPF with Customs and Excise and other branches of government failed to establish this.

There are precedents for making a levy on pension funds in order to meet certain desirable costs, and the fees of independent trustees could come into this category, so that such a person did not have to depend directly on the other trustees or the sponsoring organisation to meet their fees.

Chapter 5

Taxation, contracting-out and preservation of benefits

1. Taxation

The facts that a member of an approved occupational pension scheme obtains full tax relief on his contributions, the company recovers tax on all its contributions, and income tax deducted or capital gains realised on all UK investments is recoverable, make a pension fund the most tax-efficient form of saving that exists in the UK tax code.

When the first tax concessions were made to pension funds immediately after the Great War, a department of the Inland Revenue, the Superannuation Funds Office (now called the Pension Schemes Office, or PSO), was given the job of ensuring that pension schemes meet the requirements to qualify for tax concessions.

For each approved occupational pension scheme there must be someone who is called an administrator, to whom both the PSO and OPB can refer any queries, and indeed it is the administrator who will be the person these authorities will hold responsible for making sure that their requirements are observed.

As far as the PSO is concerned, it is their job to supervise the running of those pension funds which are granted tax approval. Since the first tax approvals were granted, not only have there been numerous Acts of Parliament, consolidating Acts and Regulations, but the PSO has also acted under discretionary powers. This arrangement has given rise to a whole set of precedents which are set out in what are known as the PSO Practice Notes. There are well over 100 pages of these practice notes, divided up into 22 parts plus 5 Appendices.

There has always been automatic approval for funds which could match the most stringent tests, but most approvals follow the use of the PSO discretion.

The Civil Service pension scheme, although it is an unfunded, pay-as-you-go system, was adopted as the model for tax approval.

The basic requirements for approval have not changed a great deal over the years, although they are set out in full in the Practice Notes, published as IR 12(1991), issued in September 1991, a copy of which is obtainable from the PSO at a cost of £10. Set out below are the main headings into which the Practice Notes are divided. This gives some idea of the wide range of matters with which the PSO is concerned.

Part 1   Introduction
Part 2   Establishment of Schemes
Part 3   Membership of Schemes
Part 4   Contributions by Employees
Part 5   Contributions by Employers Part 6 Retirement
Part 6   Retirement
Part 7   Total Benefits on Retirement
Part 8   Lump sum Benefits
Part 9   Increases of Pensions in Payment
Part 10   Leaving Pensionable Service
Part 11   Benefits on Death in Service
Part 12   Benefits on Death after Retirement
Part 13   Funding and Surpluses
Part 14   Discontinuance of Schemes
Part 15   Overseas Employers and Employees
Part 16   Administration of Schemes
Part 17   Tax Treatment of Approved Schemes
Part 18   Application for Approval
Part 19   Withdrawal for Approval
Part 20   Small Self-Administered Schemes
Part 21   Centralised Schemes
Part 22   Simplified Defined Contribution Schemes
Appendix I   Glossary of Terms
Appendix II   Forms including Prescribed Forms
Appendix III   Continued Rights
Appendix IV   Split Service
Appendix V   Part-time/Full-time Service

The more common restrictions set out in the Practice Notes are as follows:

(a) Members' benefits

Members' benefits may not exceed:

(i)   *At normal retirement date* (NRD), a pension equal to two-thirds final pay after forty years' service giving rise to the well-known fraction of one-sixtieth of final pay for each year of service (but the 1989 budget limited new schemes established after 1 June 1989, or new members of old schemes who joined after 5 April 1989, to have their final pay limited to £60,000 p.a., such figure to be escalated annually in line with price increases). (At 6 April 1991 the 'cap' became £71,400 p.a. and at 6 April 1992 £75,000 p.a.). In the March 1993 budget no escalation was given and from April 1994 the figure becomes £76,800 p.a. In the 1987 Budget the Chancellor introduced the need to average, over a period of at least the final three years, pay in excess of £100,000 p.a. This was retrospective.

It is possible to enhance the fractions for short service employees. Since 1987, a full pension may be paid after as little as twenty years' service so that a scheme's rules may apply two-sixtieths for each year of service with a maximum of twenty years to count.

Members of schemes established before April 1987 who were members before that date can receive 'enhanced' pensions on a rather different basis as shown below:

Years	Number of Sixtieths
6	8
7	16
8	24
9	32
10	40

(ii) *Cash commutation:* An amount equal to three-eightieths of final pay for each year of service may be paid, free of tax, in lieu of pension. Either a fixed conversion rate (for example, £9 cash equals £1 p.a. pension) or the strict actuarial rate may be used. There is an enhancement provision for the full one and a half year's pay level to be reached after twenty years so long as it is in line with pension 'enhancement'. The £60,000 rule applies for pensions, giving a £90,000 maximum post-1989 (from 6 April 1991, £107,100; 6 April 1992, £112,500 and £115,200 from April 1994). There is a post-1987 limit of £150,000.

Again, there are different rules for schemes established before April 1987. For members in these schemes it is not necessary to limit commutation enhancement in line with pension enhancement and the following fractions may be used:

Number of –

Years	80ths	Years	80ths
9	30	15	72
10	36	16	81
11	42	17	90
12	48	18	99
13	54	19	108
14	63	20	120

(iii) *Dependants' pensions* may not, in total, exceed the member's pension and a widow's, widower's pension or any other individual benefit may not exceed two-thirds the member's pension.

(iv) *Lump sum death benefits* may not exceed:
● in service — four times salary plus a return of member's contributions
● in retirement — £1,000.

(b) *Contributions*

Contributions by the employer must not exceed 15% of pay in a final pay scheme (there are more generous levels allowed for personal pensions; these levels start at 17.5% and rise steadily so that at age sixty-one, 40% may be paid).

Contributions by the employer must be at such a level as would not provide an overfunding in excess of 5% of the assets. (In a personal pension scheme there can be no employer contribution.)

(c) Retained benefits

Retained benefits are those arising from an earlier employment, and include the pension value of any commutation.

There are rules for bringing into account benefit with a previous employer so that it is not possible, for example, to work for twenty years for each of two employers and earn two-thirds final pay from each of them. Worse still would be the possibility of taking away more than one commuted sum.

If a pension scheme provides benefits at an annual rate beyond one-sixtieth of final pay for each year of service retained benefits must be brought into account. Since the introduction of the 'cap' the effect of retained benefits has been most marked.

(d) Unapproved pensions

The Finance Act 1989 introduced the concept of unapproved pensions which may be provided over and above the PSO limits. The thinking behind the 'capping' of approval to a salary limit of £60,000 p.a. (increasing annually in line with the Retail Prices Index) was that there must be a ceiling to the tax advantages. By introducing the possibility of saving above this ceiling without the tax advantage (but without the disadvantage of having no approval) this new concept was introduced. Provided there is no fund, taxation will arise only on payment of benefits. This seems to be a very unsatisfactory solution to the problems of the salary cap because the member does not have the security of the benefits being funded in a separate trust. The member would have to rely on the company's promise to pay the benefit from profits and, of course, the company may itself fail.

2. Contracting-out

The concept of allowing 'suitable' occupational pension schemes to take over responsibility for dealing with the earnings-related element of the State scheme was first established by the 1959 Act as a way of transferring responsibilities from the State to the private sector. The pensions legislation brought in by Keith Joseph and enacted in 1973 brought into operation the Occupational Pensions Board (OPB). Their job is to supervise the contracting-out arrangements (already dealt with in Chapter 1 in a general way), to supervise the preservation requirements (dealt with in Chapter 9) and to be a point of reference on pension questions to which the Secretary of State may refer. Unfortunately, the OPB does not operate under such wide discretionary powers as the PSO and there are therefore no practice notes as such. What there are, however, are memoranda prepared by the OPB or PSO (or, until they split up in July 1991, joint memoranda), which set out the way in which certain matters are to be treated.

Here again these points are much too detailed for consideration in a book of this sort, suffice it to say that there have been over 100 issued, some withdrawn, some amending others.

Appendix 6 (page 120) lists all memoranda extant at July 1991.

It may be worth mentioning that there is a publication setting out in full all necessary Acts, Regulations and memoranda, published by Butterworth, and available through the National Association of Pension Funds.

There are some guiding pointers which can be shortly stated.

(a) Contracting-out a final pay scheme

In essence, the employer has to show that he has an occupational pension scheme which will provide at least as good a benefit to members as they would otherwise expect from SERPS. These guaranteed minimum pensions (GMPs) can be stated briefly to be one-eightieth of pay in the Upper Earnings Band for the member, and a widow's guaranteed minimum pension (WGMP) for the widow of a member who dies before State retirement date. For more about SERPS and guaranteed minimum pensions, see pages 54–55 and 66–67.

There are requirements to maintain these GMPs and WGMPs for leavers. If a member leaves employment after less than two years then he or she may be 'bought back' into SERPS by the payment of a contribution equivalent premium (CEP). For a member who leaves having completed two years' service or more, the GMP and WGMP must be escalated up to State retirement date in one of the following ways:

(i)   by 7% per annum;

(ii) by what are known as section 21 orders (that is an annual percentage equal to the percentage rise in earnings); or

(iii) by 5% per annum and the payment of a limited revaluation premium (LRP) in consideration for which SERPS will be responsible for any annual increases beyond 5% p.a.

SERPS is responsible for the escalation of GMPs and WGMPs after State retirement date, except that since April 1988 contracted-out funds have had to provide the first 3% p.a.

WGMPs now have to be provided for potential widowers as well as widows.

(b) Contracting-out a money purchase scheme

This process is altogether simpler. To obtain a contracting-out certificate, it is only necessary to guarantee to pay into the scheme the rebate of contributions (1993 – 1996 4.8% Upper Band Earnings). There are no requirements to provide a particular level of benefit.

3. Preservation

On the completion of two years' pensionable service a member who leaves employment must be awarded a deferred pension, a transfer to a new employer's scheme or a transfer to a personal pension policy.

From 1 January 1991, the benefit in respect of the whole of such a member's service must be subject to limited price indexation (LPI) (see page 7).

For more about what happens on a change of employment, see Chapter 9.

Chapter 6

The cost

One of the most immediate questions which members of pension schemes ask is how much they are expected to contribute. This question must be broken into two parts because the State scheme is different in nearly all respects from a company pension scheme.

1. The State scheme

(a) Member's social security contributions

Although I have already run over the general arrangements, it is worth repeating the most important facts when discussing the detail, for completeness.

The first area to map out is your earnings. If you earn less than the Lower Earnings Limit (LEL) you need pay nothing to the State scheme.

LEL is roughly equal to the single person's State Flat Rate Benefit (SFRB) and for the year commencing 6 April 1994 is £57 a week or £2,964 per year. It is adjusted each year in line with the Retail Prices Index. You pay contributions if you earn more than the LEL on earnings up to the Upper Earnings Limit (UEL) but not on earnings above this point. UEL is roughly 7.5 times LEL (from April 1994, £430 a week or £22,360 per year). It too is adjusted each year.

There are certain exceptions, but normally you will pay at a rate of 2% of your earnings up to the LEL and 10% of your earnings between the LEL and the UEL. These are called Class I rates of contribution. (There is a 1.8% rebate on the 10% contribution for employees in contracted-out employment — see below.)

Exceptions are employees working abroad, who may elect to pay a fixed weekly rate (£5.55 a week from 6 April 1994), called Class III contributions. This ensures their rights to the SFRB. The same is true of those earning less than LEL.

Certain married women who made an election before May 1977 to pay a reduced fixed weekly rate (April 1994 — 3.85%), may continue to do so until their marital status changes or they cease to be employed for two consecutive tax years, or they elect to pay Class I. The so-called 'reduced rate' gives entitlement to no pension benefits and women paying this rate rely on their husbands' record for SFRB. For those earning less than £74 a week (£81 if contracted-out)in the tax year commencing 6 April 1994 the 'reduced' rate contribution is more expensive than the Class I rate!

(b) Members contracted-out of the State earnings-related scheme

If your occupational pension scheme is contracted-out of the SERPS, there is a reduction in the contribution payable which, between April 1993 and April 1996, is equal to 1.8% of earnings between the Lower Earnings Limit and the Upper Earnings Limit. It was intended that the contribution reduction would be lowered each five years, but a three-year period was chosen in 1993 so that consideration could be given to revising the whole system to make it age relative.

(c) Examples of social security contributions

If the UEL is taken at £430 a week and the LEL £57 a week then this would mean that if you earn £157 a week and you are not contracted-out, you will pay contributions of £11.14 a week. If you are contracted-out you will pay £9.34 a week. If you earn £430 a week or more and you are not contracted-out you will be paying social security contributions of £38.44 a week, but if you are contracted-out you will pay £31.73 a week.

All these contributions are assessed weekly and are strictly speaking, due each Monday, although it is accepted that payment will be made on the payroll date and this may be weekly or monthly.

(d) Employment after retirement age

Until the State pension ages are equalised, a process not due to be completed for 26 years, a man who reaches age sixty-five or a woman who reaches age sixty will automatically be entitled to a State pension subject to a sufficient contribution history. (This is 44 years for a man and 39 years for a woman but it will become 44 years for all in the year 2020). The employee does, however, have a choice. A woman upon reaching sixty, or a man reaching sixty-five, may elect to draw the pension from those ages (whether or not employment is to continue), or to defer drawing it for up to five years. Where employment continues, social security contributions by the employer only will also continue for up to five years more in each case. The benefit, increased because of the delayed payment, is then paid in all cases.

Where a man retires at sixty-five or a woman retires at sixty and draws SFRB but then takes another job at a later date, it is possible to ask for the State benefit to be stopped, thereby increasing the benefit when it restarts again. The reason for doing this is to keep the tax bill down.

By adding SFRB to earnings, you could find yourself paying tax at a higher rate.

The increase is earned week by week and is worth about 7% per annum. The option to stop drawing the SFRB can be exercised only once, and the stoppage must be for at least seven weeks before any increment is earned. As part of the equalisation proposals the annual rate of increase would become 10% and the five year deferral period would become indefinite.

(e) Self-employed persons

There are other arrangements for self-employed persons; in the broadest of terms, the same sort of contributions are required, but no benefits are earned other than the SFRB.

(f) Summary

To sum up the State social security contribution position for an employee, there are the following classes of contributor:

Class I   contributions depend upon the level of the employee's earnings as follows:

Earnings (per week)	% Contributions	
	Contracted-in	Contracted-out
Less than £57	nil	nil
Where earnings are £57 and above:		
on the first £57	2	2
on the next £373	10	8.2

Class II   this is a fixed rate contribution (subject to exemption when profits are below £3,200 per year) payable by the self-employed irrespective of their profits: £5.65 a week (April 1994).

Class III is a fixed rate contribution which may be paid by those whose earnings do not reach the LEL, who are unemployed or who are employed abroad and have no UK earnings: £5.55 a week (April 1994).

Class IV is paid by self-employed persons at a rate of 7.3% which is levied on the profits which they make each year between £6,491 and £22,360 (April 1994).

2. Occupational pension schemes

(a) Members' contributions

Now what about contributions to company pension schemes? The National Association of Pension Funds completes a survey each year covering several million members of occupational pension schemes. The 1992 survey shows that in 75% of schemes a contribution by the member is called for and that the average rate is 4.7% of pensionable earnings. This term, 'pensionable earnings', is a very important one for both contribution and benefit purposes.

(b) Pensionable earnings

Exclusions from earnings: If we start with total earnings, there may be certain exclusions to be taken into account to arrive at pensionable earnings. The first exclusion relates to the characteristics of the scheme. For example, it may be that overtime earnings or special bonuses are excluded. As the majority of overtime tends to be performed by people in their younger or middle years, the view is often taken that it would be wrong to make these earnings liable to contributions if overtime has ceased and is not available to be used to assess benefits at retirement age. The counter argument is that the level of the pension should reflect the standard of living which the member had enjoyed and therefore to exclude any earnings may depress the pension of some members, particularly those whose earnings are well above the level of SFRB.

The other exclusion which is found in a large number of schemes is calculated by reference to the SFRB. If we take this as being £57 a week, then the argument runs that the first £57 of earnings produces a 100% pension from the SFRB. In this extreme case, to offer membership of an occupational pension scheme would be totally unnecessary. Even for someone who was earning, say £85 a week the SFRB would provide a pension equal to two-thirds of earnings. There is also a point that when we talk about two-thirds of earnings we are comparing gross pension with gross pay. When we come to deal with benefits we shall see that we should really be comparing the income (after tax and other deductions) before and after retirement and this brings about a very different result indeed — more favourable to the employee.

To exclude an amount equal to the SFRB (or sometimes equal to one and a half times the SFRB) from total pay before making the contribution calculation is rather the same as the contracting-out arrangements, but in reverse. When we speak of contracting-out of SERPS we are saying that the occupational pension scheme provides the pension which SERPS would otherwise provide, and therefore the contribution to and the benefit from SERPS are excluded.

Because the target pension after a full career of service in a final pay scheme is usually two-thirds of pay, then in order to take full account of the SFRB it is necessary to exclude from the contribution and benefit calculation in the occupational pension scheme an amount equal to one and a half times the SFRB. Let us consider an example. Suppose total pay is £150 a week and the objective of the occupational pension scheme is to provide a pension (inclusive of State pension) of two-thirds total pay after forty years' service. We know the SFRB (for a single person) is £57 a week so that the occupational scheme needs to provide the difference between this figure and £100 (being two-thirds of £150, or £43 a week). This is achieved by using a formula which says that a member's pension will be one-sixtieth of his pensionable earnings, pensionable earnings being total earnings less one and a half times the SFRB.
In this example, therefore, the calculation is as follows:

$$1/60\text{th} \times £150 - £85 \text{ a week x } 40$$
$$= 40/60 \text{ x } £65 \text{ a week}$$
$$= 2/3 \text{ x } £65 = £42 \text{ a week}$$

Additions to earnings: There are some non-standard additions to members' contributions in some occupational pension schemes. Sometimes an extra 0.5% or so is required to be paid by male members who are married in order to qualify for a widow's pension. This is less likely now that widowers' pensions are a common feature of pension funds. A 'single sex' arrangement would now almost certainly be regarded as discriminatory.

In some schemes there is also an increase in contributions for people who are above the average age at entry. It may be, for example, that those over 45 are required to pay an extra 0.5%; those over 50, 1% and those over 55, 1.5%. In most schemes there is a maximum age after which an employee cannot join the pension scheme at all. The reason for having an increased contribution where a member joins at a later age is that there are fewer years over which the contributions are going to be earning investment income whereas the benefits are usually expressed as a percentage of earnings, irrespective of the age of joining the scheme.

(d) Enhanced benefits

In order to assist those who join the company with only a few years to retirement, the Pension Schemes Office has:

(i)   allowed pension scheme rules to pay 'enhanced' benefits, so that it is possible to pay a two-thirds pension after only twenty years, for example, (after only ten years for members who were members of schemes before 1987); and

(ii) allowed members in receipt of taxable non-income items such as car allowances, medical expense scheme subscriptions and accommodation allowances, to include such items for pension purposes if the scheme rules permit.

(e) Additional voluntary contributions

For the same reasons the PSO has allowed members to pay Additional Voluntary Contributions (AVCs) in order to increase the scale benefits under their schemes. Although most occupational pension schemes have benefits based on pay at or near retirement, the AVC usually goes to earn benefits on the money purchase principle. This means that the benefit which emerges depends solely upon the amount of money put in and the investment earnings which have been recorded against it. In no circumstances will the PSO allow a member of a final pay scheme to pay more than 15% of his earnings into an occupational pension scheme and this 15% must include any contributions which he makes to the scheme other than through the AVC arrangement. So in a scheme with a 5% members' contribution on earnings over and above SFRB, the member will be able to pay an AVC equal to 15% on earnings below SFRB and a further 10% on earnings above SFRB.

There are, of course, other reasons besides joining the occupational pension scheme late in a member's career, which may lead a member to decide to pay AVCs. These reasons will include:

- having a better opportunity, financially, to retire before the normal retirement date of the scheme. PSO restrictions on early retirement benefits have, until 1989, been a deterrent, however;
- being in a position to increase the pension, once it has begun, to meet any loss of purchasing power through the effects of inflation; and
- saving in the most tax efficient way possible.

3. Employers' contributions

(a) State scheme

What does an employer contribute? Generally speaking there will be some sort of relationship between the contribution made by the member and the contribution made by his employing company.

As far as the State is concerned, an employer is required to pay the full Class I contribution for all employees and that includes those who are not paying contributions themselves (because they are over retirement date or because they are married women who have exercised the option to pay at the 'lower rate' of contributions).

The company Class I contribution is rather different from that paid by the employee. There is no ceiling; no UEL for the company. On the other hand, the reduction in the employee's contribution where an employee is contracted-out is higher — 3% from April 1994.

The company pays no contribution for an employee whose earnings are below the LEL, but then pays 3.6% for those whose earnings are between £57 and £99.99 a week; 5.6% up to £145 a week; 7.6% up to £200 a week and 10.2% for those with higher earnings. There is another noticeable difference and that is in the case of someone who has more than one job. If we assume that a man is employed at £250 a week in his main job and yet earns another £250 a week in a subsidiary job, then if the upper earnings limit is £430 a week he will be able to obtain a refund of contributions from the Department of Social Security at the year end (5 April). This will relate to contributions which he has made in respect of the difference between £430 and £500. Each of his employers will need to pay the full contribution and there will be no refund due to either of them.

(b) Occupational pension schemes

We have seen that in the majority of occupational pension schemes, the member will pay something like 5% of his pensionable pay. In final pay schemes the employing company is required to pay the balance of the cost, and for ease of expression, this may be stated, for example, as being twice the members' contributions, on average. This is a rather misleading piece of shorthand, however, as we shall see later when talking about early leavers. Depending upon the results of the actuarial valuation there may be a need from time to time to increase or decrease the amount which the employing company pays.

It is also possible for an occupational pension scheme to be introduced and for credit to be given for years of service prior to the introduction of the scheme. In nearly all such cases the employing company makes the contribution necessary to pay for this past service element and the costs are very often spread over a period of years. Thus, in addition to the standard contribution, the employer will also have a past service contribution which can be of a very significant amount if there are a large number of long-serving employees with the company at the time the pension scheme is introduced. A different sort of past service contribution will also arise if significant improvements are made to an existing scheme and back dated.

In the 1970s we often found a company making what is known as a special contribution. This arises where the actuary has stated that the employer's normal rate of contribution is not sufficiently high to meet the balance of liabilities and the company has decided that its profits are such that a lump sum should be paid into the pension fund rather than paying an increased annual contribution rate for the future. There are restrictions in the amount which can be paid in by way of a lump sum. Normally the PSO will only give tax relief if the special contribution is no greater that the normal annual contribution.

Then we went through a period when companies rarely made sufficient profit to be able to consider this course. More recently we found that another combination of circumstances led to company contributions being reduced. The introduction, in 1989, of the accounting standard SSAP 24 affects the 'pace of funding' which until then, a company was free to determine itself. In fact, the amount paid to the pension fund by way of company contributions can now vary in cash terms without affecting the company's profit and loss account.

Where there is an AVC scheme, there needs to be no matching company contribution. The PSO regards the stipulation that there must always be a company contribution as being satisfied if the company meets the administrative costs of the scheme.

4. The future

(a) State scheme contributions

What about the future? Well, the State scheme is uprated annually (the SFRB rises in line with the RPI, and SERPS rises in line with wage levels generally); and the Secretary of State is required by law to review the amount of contribution which is required as from the 6 April each year. He also reviews the Lower and Upper Earnings Limit and there is always the political option of altering, usually increasing, the contribution rate itself.

The State Graduated Pension Scheme which came into effect in 1961 and closed in 1975, and the State Earnings Related Scheme which came into effect in 1978, were both variations in the way that the State collects contributions in order to meet a deficit in the amount of money available to pay immediate benefits. The State Graduated Scheme benefits are still payable, and since 1978 have been price-protected. SERPS would not have come into full maturity until 1998 had it not been varied after the first ten years in 1988. It would be a very brave observer who stated categorically that there were unlikely to be any further major changes in the State arrangements before the end of the century. The Government Actuary has already indicated that the age distribution of the working population will lead to higher contributions being required. Naturally, if benefit levels are increased this will make contributions even higher.

The Social Security Act 1986 changes to SERPS which became effective in 1988 are discussed in Chapter 1.

(b) Occupational pension schemes

Occupational pension schemes have a very long history of improvement, but improvement can only come about if more money is put into the scheme. The member's contribution rates have tended to rise from the days when a few pence or shillings were collected each week to the situation now where the contribution rate may run into many pounds a week.

I think it is only fair to say that most of the improvements in occupational pension schemes have come about as a result of the initiative of the employing companies and, because of this, the employing companies have tended to bear a disproportionate amount of the cost. In particular the past service costs which, as explained above, arise when an improvement is made retrospectively, have tended to be charged to the employing companies rather than to the members.

The Social Security Act 1986 and new Revenue regulations have led to many changes being introduced from 1988. The Social Security Act 1990 has already improved the lot of the leaver and is planned to protect the pensioner from a date yet to be announced.

5. Costs of price protection

Another cost, which in a way is a past service cost, arises from the improvement of the level of pensions in course of payment. Although the NAPF survey now shows that many schemes do include a fixed element of increase to pensions after they have commenced (the most popular annual rate of increase is 3%), any increases above the fixed levels which are awarded must be paid for. Payment has been made either in a single payment where the profits of the company allow, added to the past service charges, or the charge has been accepted by the trustees as part of the reduction in the surplus which the actuary takes into account in his next valuation.

The 1992 Survey shows that 90% of all members are in schemes with guaranteed pension reviews, but in the private sector this percentage is only 86%, whereas in the public sector it is 98%, where most people are in schemes which match rises in the Retail Prices Index (RPI).

The Social Security Act 1985 required that the deferred pensions of early leavers who left service after 1 January 1986 must increase annually in respect of post-1 January 1985 benefit, at the rate of increase in the RPI up to a maximum of 5% per year cumulatively. Before these provisions it was rare in the private sector to award any increase. For example, the NAPF 1985 Survey showed that only 6% of all schemes granted increases for deferred and current pensions on the same basis, and in the private sector 67% of schemes granted no increase at all on deferred pensions. 54% of all members of private sector schemes received no guaranteed deferred benefit increase. In the 1989 Survey 67% of all members were guaranteed increases on the whole of the deferred pension with only 15% of members limited to the statutory minimum. As we shall see later, the question of the early leaver and the erosion of the purchasing power of the deferred pension brought about by inflation led the OPB to recommend that there should be an automatic 5% per annum increase in deferred pensions. That cost was estimated by the OPB as being between 1% and 2% of payroll according to the sex distribution of the deferred benefit population. This itself was not an insignificant increase in the total cost of the scheme, but it was argued that it would be inconceivable that there would not be the same increase granted to those already receiving a pension, and the additional cost of doing this would be very much greater than the 1% or 2% quoted. The alternative to facing these very large increases in the rates of contribution would be to reduce the initial pension and then grant increases upon that lower figure. The Social Security Act 1990 did indeed introduce the requirement that all final pay schemes provide Limited Price Indexation (LPI) in respect of all service for leavers after 1 January 1991.

Guaranteed minimum pensions (GMP), the contracted-out-occupational pension scheme benefits which replace SERPS benefits, are fully indexed against increases in prices through SERPS itself after State retirement age (SRA), although contracted-out schemes have been required to increase the GMP arising after April 1988 by the first 3% p.a. rise in the RPI. For earlier leavers, between date of leaving service and SRA the GMP must be price protected by the contracted-out scheme. There are three ways of doing this. The most commonly adopted is to increase the GMP by 7% a year. This was considered the safest course to follow when inflation was at its worst. The alternative of indexing, either by matching the rises in RPI in full or up to 5% p.a. together with the payment of a premium (in exchange for which SERPS matches the

RPI above 5%) has started to look more attractive. No retrospective changes can be made, however.

The arrival on the scene of the AVC scheme paid for by the member has allowed the member very much more choice to determine the benefits he or she wants in his or her own particular circumstances rather than relying on the general pattern of benefits offered to members of the scheme as a whole. It has already been considered that one of the reasons that occupational pension schemes are more successful than the State scheme is that they can be tailored more to the needs of the individual. The AVC concept takes this idea one stage further. From 1988 all occupational pension schemes have been required to offer an AVC facility.

It was considered to be outside the scope of this book to deal with the question of self-employed person's pension arrangements or indeed policies which individuals may take out with the insurance companies to improve their income expectations after retirement. There has, however, been much comment about personal pensions from the time of the Centre for Policy Studies Report in 1983 culminating in the Social Security Act 1986. This subject is now dealt with in Chapter 14.

6. Tax reliefs on contributions

There is no tax relief for employees in respect of social security contributions. Companies, however, can set off such expenditures as they make against their profits.

Within the PSO limits set out in Chapter 5, members of occupational pension schemes are granted full tax relief on contributions. Thus employees who are contracted-out enjoy a small tax advantage. Companies, as with the State scheme contributions, enjoy a set off for occupational scheme contributions for tax purposes.

Chapter 7

Benefits on retirement

The benefits which you can expect to receive on retirement will clearly depend on quite a variety of factors. You may have been a member of one or more pension schemes; you may have saved in other ways in order to enjoy your retirement. If you have been an employee or self-employed then you will certainly be entitled to the State Flat Rate Benefit subject to contribution record.

1. The State scheme

(a) The State Flat Rate Benefit (SFRB)

So let us look at the State scheme first. Benefits are only less than the standard rate if, for some reason, the required number of national insurance contributions has not been paid or contribution credits obtained (for example, while drawing sickness benefits). The SFRB was introduced in the National Insurance Act 1946, which came into force on 5 July 1948. At that time the contributions amounted to a few pence a week and the benefit promised when the scheme reached maturity in 1958 was to be £1.30 a week (single persons' rate). By the time 1958 arrived the actual amount paid was nearly double that promised. (There were various types of State old age pension arrangements available under earlier legislation, going back to the five shillings a week Lloyd George Pension of 1908. That, however, was a means-tested pension payable only at age seventy. Before 1948 only 'manual workers' were required to belong to the State scheme.) The 1948 rules provided that so long as an employee had paid, on average, 50 contributions (or received credits) for each 'contribution year' he would be entitled to receive full benefit. A 'contribution year' is each year between 5 July 1948 (or such later date as the employee was required to contribute, currently the employee's sixteenth birthday) and State retirement age. Originally, to assist what was almost universal manual record keeping, each person's National Insurance number ended with a suffix letter A, B, C or D which determined when the contribution year ended and allowed four separate dates on which N.I. cards were to be exchanged.

The amount of the SFRB increases each year. At April 1994, it is £57.60 a week for a single person and £92.10 a week for a married couple. State retirement age has, since 1940, been age sixty-five for men and age sixty for women but is due to be equalised at sixty-five again by the year 2020.

The reason that an employee may not qualify for the full benefit, or for any at all, could be that the employee was abroad and therefore not liable to pay contributions (unless he or she was working in a country with a reciprocal social security agreement); he or she was self-employed; or elected, as a married woman, not to pay contributions.

You can ask at any office of the Department of Social Security for your contribution record and this will show your expected benefit entitlement.

(b) The State Graduated Pension Scheme 1961–1975

Another Pensions Act, passed in 1959, provided for graduated contributions to be paid from April 1961. These graduated contributions give a right to further benefits at the rate of 2.5p a week for each £15 contributed by a man and his employer or £18 contributed by a woman and her employer. Graduated contributions were payable by all employees with earnings over £9 a week. There was a ceiling, originally £15 a week, which by 1975 had become roughly twice the rate of national average earnings. It was possible for an occupational pensions scheme to 'contract-out' of part of the arrangement (described fully later in this chapter). That scheme ended in April 1975 and, if you contributed to it, you should have a small square of paper issued by the Department of Social Security which indicated the number of 2.5p a week units which you would receive from normal retirement age. The most that could have been earned was £3.32 for a man and £2.78 for a woman. To put this into context the national average wage at this time was some £50 a week. From 1978 the value of this entitlement has risen in line with the prices and at April 1994 the maximum figures were £7.48 a week for a man and £6.26 a week for a woman.

(c) The State Earnings-Related Pension Scheme 1978 (SERPS)

The Social Security Pensions Act introduced in 1975 by Mrs Barbara Castle, brought to an end, after many years of argument between the political parties, doubts about what should replace the State Graduated Scheme. SERPS came into force in April 1978 and provided additional State pension based on earnings which exceeded a 'floor' (£57 a week, April 1994) called the Lower Earnings Limit (LEL) equal to the State Flat Rate Benefit. There is also a 'ceiling' called the Upper Earnings Limit (UEL) of approximately 7.5 times the amount of the 'floor' (£430 a week, April 1994); both limits are increased each year. The amount of benefit earned under this scheme was to provide, when the scheme reached full maturity, an amount equal to one-quarter of the band of earnings on which contributions were paid (known as 'upper band earnings').

Each year's record was to be uprated, sometimes described as 'index-linked', against the rise in the wages index so that if you had been at the mid-point of the upper earnings band of every year then the earnings-related benefit would be 25% of the mid-point between LEL and UEL in your final year. In 1994 terms the mid-point was £186.50 a week so that the benefit would be 25% of £129.50 (£186.50 – £57) or £32.37 a week. There is one further complication in the scheme, namely that after 1998 the *best* twenty years were to count. If you retired between 1978 and 1998 the amount would be proportionate, that is 1.25% of the band of earnings on which contributions have been paid in respect of each year between April 1978 and State retirement age. From the year 2000, the target will become 20% and it will be all earnings, *not* the best twenty years which will count.

(d) Contracted-out schemes

Most employees who are in an occupational pension scheme are in fact 'contracted-out' of SERPS. This means that the occupational pension scheme undertakes to provide a benefit at least equal to that which would have been earned under SERPS. It is not possible to contract-out of the SFRB.

(e) Income tax on State benefits

All State benefits rank as earned income and they are therefore subject to income tax. There is, however, no procedure whereby post offices can collect tax from State benefits. Where there is other income, which brings the total income into a tax paying bracket, the collection of tax becomes the responsibility of, usually, the occupational pension scheme. State pensions can be collected weekly by order book from the post office or received monthly or quarterly in arrears, by cheque to your home address. The Government had said that arrangements would be made to deduct tax from State benefits at source from April 1983, but this proposal has been shelved.

2. Occupational pension schemes

(a) Pensions

The position as far as occupational pension schemes are concerned is very different. Most occupational pension schemes had the same normal retirement age as the State, namely sixty-five for men and sixty for women, but that was about as far as the similarities went.

The very great majority of members are in schemes which provide a pension based on pensionable earnings at or near retirement. The most frequently used basis on which pensions are calculated is to average pensionable earnings over the best three consecutive years in the last ten years of service.

Pensionable earnings may, for example, exclude overtime earnings and about half of all occupational pension schemes make some allowance for the SFRB by making a deduction from total earnings. This deduction is usually referred to as 'integration'. For example, if the SFRB equals £2,964, then the first £2,964 of earnings may be excluded both from contribution and benefit calculations in the occupational pension scheme. An employee whose total earnings are £12,964, would thus have pensionable earnings of £10,000 p.a. To line up with the target of two-thirds pension the integration should be one and a half times SFRB, but this is difficult to explain and is less often used.

Alternatively, the occupational pension may be calculated on total earnings; the figure resulting from that calculation is then reduced by an amount equal to the SFRB earned in the same period of service. Using the same example, this would mean a reduction of £85.50 for each year of a member's service. For a member with forty years' service this will result in a reduction of the full £2,964.

As occupational pension schemes were set up long before inflation became an important factor, the position of the employee who changes jobs (and indeed the employee who retires on pension) is not entirely satisfactory except in the public sector where generally benefits are 'index-linked'. Because most pensions are calculated on earnings in the last three years a member who retires after a full career starts off with a fairly good pension (but the purchasing power is then reduced each year in line with inflation). The NAPF 1992 Survey shows that 86% of members in schemes in the private sector are guaranteed increases on pensions in course of payment. Many companies grant discretionary increases in addition.

The member who leaves has the purchasing power of his deferred pension reduced in line with inflation, less the value of any increases, from the day he leaves his job. In respect of these deferred pensions the position changed from 1985 when it became mandatory to escalate such benefit up to State pension age by the percentage increase in the RPI up to 5% p.a. and again from 1 January 1991 when such increases (referred to as Limited Price Indexation (LPI)) had to be granted on benefits dating back to the commencement of the members' service. In addition, the very large majority of members of occupational pension schemes are in contracted-out schemes and the amount which has to be provided in order to qualify to contract-out will each year become a larger proportion of the total benefit. This growing part of the occupational pension will thus be virtually 'index-linked'.

(b) Commutation — exchanging part of the pension for cash

Unlike the State scheme, most occupational pension schemes will allow you to take part of your pension in cash form. There are restrictions, but if you have completed twenty years' service it is possible to take as much as one and a half times your final year's pay in a final pay scheme.

Such a cash payment is not subject to tax, but, of course, if investments are made with this money the income arising from it is subject to tax.

The amount of pension which you have to give up in exchange for the cash will vary from scheme to scheme. Typically, a man at age sixty-five will have to give up £100 a year to obtain £900 cash.

New rules for commuting personal or money purchase pensions will require that no more than about one-quarter of the emerging pension can be taken as cash.

(c) Working beyond normal retirement age

If you remain in employment beyond normal retirement date it is usual for arrangements to be made in the occupational pension scheme:

either to stop all further contributions, benefits to commence at the actual later retirement at a higher rate (to recognise the period over which the benefits were not paid);

or to continue to pay contributions and earn further scale benefits up to actual later retirement.

It is now possible to draw the benefit and continue in employment but this would give rise to a very heavy tax liability and it is not usually favoured.

A further alternative is to take the commutation but to defer the pension to actual late retirement.

(d) Early retirement

Unlike the State benefits, those under an occupational pension scheme can be drawn before normal retirement date. In this case payment will be at a lower rate (because the benefits will be paid for a longer period and less interest will have been earned).

The actuary will normally provide tables for early and late retirement.

3. Unemployment benefit and an occupational pension

Another provision applies to men who receive an occupational pension in the five years before age sixty-five. Where the occupational pension exceeds £35.00 a week unemployment benefit is reduced, in this case becoming virtually a 100% tax on the unemployment benefit. There is no corresponding provision applying to women.

4. Ill-health pensions

Where an employee is unable to continue in employment through ill-health, the State will pay sickness benefit (dependent upon the employee's contribution record) for up to three years. After that, assuming the sickness has not become invalidity, the only possible benefit will be means-tested social security payments. Most occupational pension schemes can pay an ill-health pension from any age, but the amount will depend upon the employee's expectation of life. Ill-health and redundancy are both events which are likely to be treated sympathetically by the employing company and frequently the occupational pension scheme is used as a way of allowing an older employee to retire early with a reasonable income. This will be accomplished by making additional payments into the occupational pension scheme.

5. Claiming your benefits

So how does the man approaching sixty-five or the woman approaching sixty go about securing the proper benefits? About four months before State retirement age the Department of Social Security will enquire whether you intend to retire and, if so, how you wish the benefit to be paid.

If you have moved house and you have not claimed sickness or unemployment benefit since then, your last recorded address may not be where you now live. It is as well, therefore, to advise the DSS of your new address, say, six months before State retirement age.

Your occupational pension scheme details will normally be sent to you a month or two before retirement. As most benefits will depend on earnings right up to retirement date an exact figure may not be available until after your retirement. Generally, payments will be made monthly through your bank account. Some occupational pension schemes pay in advance. If you do not have a bank account arrangements will be made to open a deposit account for you which can accept a bank transfer and from which you can draw cash.

A form will be sent to your tax office giving details of your pension benefits, but it may be a month or two before the correct deductions are made.

6. Other benefits

You would not expect a reference book of this sort to be able to go into any detail about other benefits which may be available to you by virtue of the fact that you have reached State retirement age. Some will be quite trivial but others are valuable. For example, rail fares outside the busy period are often substantially reduced. Where income is at a very low level, income support may be payable. Up to £5 a week from an occupational pension scheme will be disregarded in this connection and a rather higher figure in some special circumstances. Cash savings of up to £3,000 will also be ignored.

Chapter 8

Benefits on death

1. State benefits

(a) Lump sum

First of all let us deal with what the State pays on the death of an employee. When the National Insurance Act was passed in 1946 it was decided that there should be a death grant to enable the basic cost of the funeral to be met. Even then, the amount was hardly enough to undertake the simplest type of ceremony and the amount was only increased once to £30. If the amount of the death grant had been kept in line with inflation, then it would probably have been something like £200 by the time the Government decided that rather than increase the amount, the death grant should be abolished. Hardship cases are now dealt with from a special fund. Similarly, the allowance paid to a widow during the first twenty-six weeks of widowhood has been replaced by a lump sum of £1,000. I have suggested to more than one Minister in successive Governments that the problem might be dealt with by requiring every employed person to insure themselves for a reasonable sum to meet the costs of their funerals, in much the same way as every owner of a car is required to take out third-party insurance. Then occupational pension schemes which provide a lump sum equal to, say, more than one year's pay, as a death in service benefit could qualify as a suitable insurance. This would be an important extension of the contracting-out procedures in the earnings-related part of the State pension. (It would be necessary to have a death in retirement benefit in the occupational scheme at least equal to the cost of a funeral.)

(b) Widow's pension

Subject to contribution requirements, most widows will be entitled to pensions on the death of their husbands. It works in this way:

(i) there is a lump sum payment of £1,000, to help adjust to the new circumstances;

(ii) a widow who is age fifty-five or over will qualify for the long-term widow's pension;

(iii) a widow with dependent children under age nineteen will qualify for widow's pension;

(iv) a widow who is forty-five but not fifty-five without dependent children under nineteen, will qualify for a reduced long-term widow's pension, while a widow who is fifty-five when the dependent child qualification ends will receive the full pension.

These benefits commence from the date of the employee's death. The widow's pension is increased where there are dependent children, according to the number of children involved.

There will also be additions to the widow's pension where the deceased employee had been entitled to a benefit under the State Graduated Pension Scheme which ran between 1961 and 1975. The amount is equal to one-half of the annual amount which stood to his credit at the date of his death and to which he would have become entitled at age sixty-five.

There is also a further widow's pension where the employee had not been contracted-out of SERPS. The position here is that the widow inherits the full rights to the earnings-related pension which stood to the credit of her late husband at the date of his death and to which he would have become entitled at age 65. Although the total amount due is not very large at present, it will ultimately represent an amount equal to 25% of the employee's earnings in the upper earnings band. The 1986 Act provides that only one-half of the member's SERPS pension will be inherited by a widow on the death of a member after the year 2000.

The widow's pension under the State Flat Rate Benefit is adjusted each year. The amount under the State Graduated Scheme was fixed at the date the scheme terminated in 1975 but this amount is adjusted in line with the State Flat Rate Benefit from 1978 onwards. The SERPS widow's pension is also adjusted each year after it comes into payment.

2. Occupational pension schemes

(a) Lump sum

Once again the arrangements under an occupational pension scheme are really very different. There is usually a lump sum death benefit amounting to, typically, two years' pay; in fact the PSO will allow an amount equal to four times annual pay to be paid as a lump sum death in service benefit. Where death takes place after retirement the PSO will allow a payment of up to £1,000 provided the deceased member had been a member of the pension scheme prior to 1 October 1991.

If this payment were made to the estate of the deceased member then, if the beneficiary was not the spouse, there would be the risk of Inheritance Tax having to be paid. To avoid this situation most pension schemes are arranged so that the lump sum benefit is paid at the discretion of the trustees to a range of beneficiaries which will probably include:

- the widow or widower
- the dependent children of the member
- other dependants
- other relatives
- persons named in the member's will or nomination form
- the legal personal representatives of the member.

Provided that the trustees exercise this discretion as to whom they pay the benefits within twenty-four months of the member's death, then there will be no liability to Inheritance Tax. The term 'paid at discretion of the trustees' does not mean that the trustees can sit down and decide whether or not to pay the amount; it merely means they have the discretion to choose whom should receive the benefits or perhaps share the benefits.

In larger schemes, as I explained in Chapter 3, it is quite often the case that employing company committees or locally based committees are set up to deal with the question of choosing beneficiaries in the event of a death in service, under powers delegated to them by the trustees. The matter of the security of the information that is passed to them in order for them to make a decision is stressed because it is important that all the facts are placed before them and at times, some delicate situations will be revealed. The *Consultative Document on Divorce,* mentioned in Chapter 14, would have a bearing.

(b) Nomination forms

The member may assist the trustees, or the appropriate committee, in coming to their decision by leaving what is sometimes referred to as a 'wish letter', in which he will set out the way in which he would like the trustees to exercise their discretion. The reason for expressing matters in this rather roundabout way is that the trustees may not be directed or their discretion will become what is known as 'fettered' which may jeopardise the tax position. A typical 'wish letter' is set out in Appendix 4 (page 117). Members are invited to lodge such a form in a sealed envelope with the member's name and the date it was lodged on the outside. It would be opened only in the event of the member's death or returned to him unopened upon his request. Unlike a Will, it is not necessary for a wish letter to be witnessed.

(c) Management Committee questionnaire

It is often easier to obtain an idea of what administrative arrangements are necessary by looking at an example of one particular pension fund's methods. Drafts of a questionnaire to help trustees exercise their discretion over death benefits, and a draft recommendation as to how that discretion should be exercised, are set out in Appendices 7 and 8 (page 123 *et seq*).

(d) Widows' pensions

All contracted-out schemes, and there are over ten million members in contracted-out schemes, must include provision, on death in service of a male member, for a widow's pension (up to widow's Guaranteed Minimum Pension level — which is equal to 1/160th of upper band earnings for each year of contracted-out service). It is now necessary (in respect of benefits arising after April 1988) to include a widower's pension in the case of a female member. More and more occupational pension schemes have made provision for widower's pension where there is some dependency.

It is probably the case that if we were starting from today, most occupational schemes would provide a widow's pension or widower's pension only where there is dependency. Because pension arrangements were set up when, almost by definition, a widow was dependent, dependency was not made a requirement. It would be extremely difficult to make that sort of change now when so many potential widows have acquired contingent rights.

Widow's/widower's pensions are normally related to the member's anticipated pension (based on pay at death, but service to what would have been normal retirement date) and the most common fraction to be found is one-half. The PSO will allow widow's/widower's pensions to be as much as two-thirds of the member's anticipated pension.

The Lord Chancellor's Office has issued a consultative document on *Divorce and Occupational Pension Schemes* which would have far-reaching implications. The paper is discussed in Chapter 14.

(e) Other dependants

An occupational pension scheme has much more flexibility than the State scheme in that it can choose as a beneficiary a person other than the widow (where, for example, the widow was not living with or supported by the member at the date of his death). There will also be cases where the trustees consider that it would be more appropriate to select someone else as being dependent on the deceased member. Although the most obvious alternative will be a common-law widow, there may well be cases where there is a dependent elderly parent or other relation whom the trustees would select instead of the legal (but not dependent) widow.

This is apart from cases where there may be dependants and no widow or widower. The PSO will allow pensions to dependants to be paid provided that in total the amount of such pension is not greater than the member's anticipated pension. It could be the case that there is a widow's pension of two-thirds the member's expected pension and a child allowance equal to one-third the member's expected pension or any other variant which the trustees may choose, provided the trust deed gives them power.

(f) Increases in pensions for widows and other dependants

The question of increases in the benefits under an occupational pension scheme after payment has begun is not nearly so clear cut as with the State scheme arrangements. There are schemes which include certain automatic increases to dependants' pensions but these are usually restricted to the same sort of levels as increases to pensioners themselves; the most common figure used is 3% per annum.

Where employing companies have granted increases over and above the fixed amounts on an *ad hoc* basis, dependants' pensions have nearly always been included.

3. A member's Will

Members often ask about the status of a Will in relation to benefits arising under their pension scheme. First of all, it should be noted that the trustees are not bound to observe the conditions of a Will, but they may regard it as a helpful indication. This cannot always be taken to be the case because it may not be clear from the wording of the Will whether the member expected the trustees to take his Will into account or not. This is another reason why it is helpful if the member lodges a 'wish letter' (see Appendix 4 page 117) with the trustees making it quite clear what he would like the trustees to take into consideration and how he would like them to decide to make payments.

Chapter 9

Benefits on leaving an employer

1. State schemes

(a) General

Benefits under the State scheme are not affected by a change of employer. Everyone in employment is required to contribute to the State scheme (unless their earnings are below the Lower Earnings Limit — £57 a week, 1994 level), and all employers are required similarly to make contributions. It is the employer who has to deduct the appropriate contributions from employees. There is, as a result, no loss or gain in the benefit levels which can be anticipated by an employee no matter how often he changes jobs. Obviously, if the change in jobs brings about a change in earnings the earnings-related part of the State scheme benefit will alter but no differently from a change in earnings with the same employer.

The position under the State scheme is affected, however, if leaving one employer is not followed by joining another. There can be a number of reasons why this should be the case and the results are different.

(b) Leaving employment and becoming unemployed

If an employee becomes unemployed then in normal circumstances there will be an entitlement under the State scheme to the short-term benefit known as unemployment benefit. Normally the fact that unemployment benefit is paid will mean that a credit is given to the individual in respect of his social security record. If the unemployment benefit is not claimed, a credit will not be established, except in the case of a man who is aged between sixty and sixty-five.

It may be worth mentioning here that short-term benefits, like unemployment or sickness benefit, have not been subject to income tax. This means that when an employee becomes unemployed it is usually the case that there will be a refund of the income tax which was paid while in employment in the earlier part of that tax year. The amount depends on the time of the year in which the unemployment commenced.

(c) Becoming self-employed

If an employee leaves an employer to become self-employed, then he will not have the opportunity to earn any further earnings-related social security benefits. A self-employed person will be required to pay the Class II and Class IV rates of contribution, described in Chapter 1, from the time of becoming self-employed.

(d) Leaving the UK

Another reason for an employee leaving an employer is that he wishes to go abroad. From the benefit point of view he will have to rely on his contribution record for both flat rate and earnings-related benefits. As far as contributions are concerned, he need pay no contributions to the State scheme at all. Voluntarily, he may pay the Class III contributions, described in Chapter 1, which will maintain his position for certain of the long-term benefits. There are a number of reciprocal agreements on social security with the EC and other countries which may be useful to an employee moving to one of these countries.

2. Occupational schemes

(a) General

As far as occupational pension schemes are concerned the position is once again very different. Where someone is moving around within the public sector, then really there is not a change of employer at all and there are arrangements referred to as the public sector transfer club where years of service in one public sector industry may be assumed in another public sector industry without any loss of benefits at all. Much the same situation arises when someone moves around from one employing company to another within the same group of companies. In this latter case, there is not the machinery of a transfer club; the member merely remains within the same scheme but a different employing company assumes responsibility for paying over the contributions to the trustees.

When an employee moves within the private sector from one group to another, however, the position is not nearly so satisfactory from the individual's point of view in a final pay scheme, which at present is by far the most commonly found. The Pensions Act 1973 made preservation compulsory from 1975 onwards. Under this Act, in respect of service after 5 April 1975, a member of a pension scheme who had completed five years' service in that scheme could not receive a refund of contributions on leaving one employer to join another unless he was under age twenty-six. Before 1975, a member of a pension scheme irrespective of age or service, could elect to have back all the contributions which he had made to his occupational pension scheme subject to a 10% tax deduction. If he had been a member of an occupational pension scheme contracted-out of the State graduated pension scheme, then there was also the requirement to preserve what was known as the Equivalent Pension Benefit.

In this way, the contracted-out employee did not stand in a less favourable position, at normal retirement date, than an employee who had not been contracted-out.

After SERPS came into force in 1978 an employee with less than five years' service under age twenty-six (the age qualification was removed by the 1985 Act) could still elect for a refund of contributions, still with a 10% tax deduction. Any employee, irrespective of age or service, who has been a member of a contracted-out scheme must have preserved for him what is known as the Guaranteed Minimum Pension (GMP). This is very similar in form to the old Equivalent Pension Benefit under the State Graduated Scheme. Because SERPS embraces a much broader band of earnings and provides a potentially greater benefit, then the contracted-out element is similarly larger. The GMP, therefore, will exceed the Equivalent Pension Benefit for most employees by a substantial margin. (In respect of service after April 1978 there may be very little left by way of a refund where a refund is permitted.)

From April 1988, it is not possible to receive a refund after only two years' membership of a pension scheme.

(b) Preservation of GMP

Preservation can be achieved in a contracted-out scheme in one of three ways:

(i) Where an employee has less than two years' pensionable service, it is possible to make a payment to SERPS in order to 'buy back' the individual into SERPS, thus relieving the occupational pension arrangement of any further liability for GMP.

(ii) It is possible to transfer the liability to another occupational pension scheme.

(iii) A deferred pension can be provided within the occupational pension scheme which the member is leaving but the GMP must be uprated in one of three ways:
   - by 7% each year,
   - by the percentage increase in Retail Prices Index up to 5% each year, together with a payment of a Limited Revaluation Premium to SERPS which will make good the difference between 5% and increases in the earnings index above 5% (see below); or
   - by keeping the pension roughly in line with increases in earnings (specifically in line with what are known as section 21 orders).

In most schemes there will be a pension larger than the original GMP to be preserved. Let us say that at the time the employee leaves the employment of the employer in question, he has a deferred pension of £500 a year of which £100 is the GMP.

Originally it was possible to adopt a practice known as 'franking' which meant that if, by the time the deferred pensioner reached retirement age, the GMP had become say £300 p.a., then, because the deferred pensioner was in total being paid more than £300 p.a., the overall pension of £500 p.a. did not have to be increased. The 'anti-franking' legislation which came into force 1 January 1985 (fully described in *NAPF Notes on Pensions* No. 14) stopped the practice, but only in respect of those leaving after 31 December 1984.

From 1 January 1986 leavers' benefits in excess of GMP in respect of service after 1 January 1985 had to be escalated by the lower of 5% p.a. cumulative or the annual percentage rise in prices. This arrangement now known as Limited Price Indexation or LPI very closely follows an OPB recommendation in which they estimated the cost as between 1% and 2% of payroll. Rather ingenuously the Goverment said it would make no provisions about who should pay the cost. The only alternative to the employers' increasing their contributions is for members to pay, or for benefits to be appropriately reduced; both rather unlikely possibilities.

From 1 January 1991 leavers' benefits in excess of GMP in respect of all service have had to be subjected to LPI.

(c) Transfer arrangements

In the Finance Act 1981, section 32 provided that a member leaving a pension fund could ask the trustees to transfer his entitlement to an insurance company who would provide a deferred annuity. There were a number of problems associated with such a concept.

First, the trustees were not protected against the failure of the insurance company to pay the benefit. This was corrected by new legislation effective 1 January 1986 from which date it has been mandatory for the trustees to offer a transfer value including a section 32 transfer.

Secondly, the insurance companies can quote for 'with profits' policies where there is a very small guaranteed pension and a great deal of hope. Cumulative interest, if achieved at very high levels, can translate relatively small sums to huge amounts over a long term. Pension funds, because they are generally based on final pay and because they have always ranked prudent investment management very highly, have assumed realistic rates of growth and not amended those assumptions to deal with fluctuations either up or down. Thus, if a member aged forty earning £20,000 p.a. has built up ten years' pension at one-sixtieth of his pay less one and a half times SFRB his deferred pension will be:

$$10/60 \times (£20,000 - £4,446) = £2,592 \text{ p.a.}$$

with a capital value at that time of, say £3,667.

If the deferred pension is payable twenty years hence, the current capital value on a 9% p.a. interest assumption would be some £20,000. An insurance company salesman, wanting the sale to boost his commission earnings or to give him the lead in a competition providing him with two weeks in St. Lucia, may well quote the possibility of translating that transfer value into £40,000 using a build-up of 12% p.a. to give a pension of over twice as much. If in fact less than 9% is achieved, the deferred pensioner will end up with a smaller pension, but that is twenty years away.

Naturally, pension fund administrators will advise their trustees that leaving members will be open to such exploitation and consequently the actuary is now being asked to make assumptions much closer to market rates, in fairness to the members who do not leave. The deferred pensions will remain unaltered but during times of high investment earnings potential the transfer values will be lower.

At least progress has been made in one area as a result of the Social Security Act 1990. At last a Registry of Pension Funds has been established at the DSS in Newcastle upon Tyne, to act as a tracing agency. All funds are required to register and to pay a levy to finance the operation. While this might not do much to help current deferred pensioners find their trustees, it should stop the problem becoming any worse.

(d) The future

The subject of the early leaver is a complex one. It must be remembered that pension funds were designed at a time when:

- the employee who changed jobs at all was regarded with some suspicion; he lacked stability, loyalty; he was an altogether doubtful quantity;
- inflation meant putting air into bicycle tyres or blowing up a football;
- interest rates were 2−3% p.a.
- the receipt of a pension was a reward for diligent life-long service with one employer; and
- the Welfare State had not been dreamed of.

The position we now find ourselves in is very different:

- job mobility is regarded as good for the economy;
- many employees have been forced to change jobs by redundancy;
- high and sustained price inflation has eaten into all forms of savings, not least deferred pensions in occupational schemes;
- interest rates have been in double figures for most of the last few years; and
- the widespread benefits under State schemes have increased expectations rather than satisfied needs.

So how can occupational pension schemes be realigned? If there were no shortage of resources it would be easy. There would be higher contributions to enable deferred pensions awarded to leavers (and current pensions awarded to those who retired) to be increased to retain their purchasing power. But inflation has also brought in its train recession. Employers are trying to reduce costs, not increase them. Employees are also caught in the financial squeeze with less opportunity to earn overtime or progress to jobs with higher pay — so they are not in the best position to find extra contributions.

Nevertheless, there has been much legislation awarding the early leaver increased benefit. The 1973 Act required preservation for those with five years' service or more; franking of benefits, whereby the balance over the GMP could be effectively reduced, has been stopped and from 1 January 1986 deferred benefits earned after 1 January 1985 have had to be uplifted annually by the lower of the Index of Retail Prices or a cumulative 5%. This was taken further from 1 January 1991 after which all service of a leaver had to be subject to Limited Price Indexation.

(e) The job-changer who is head-hunted

Some individuals may have the opportunity of negotiating with a new employer some rearrangement of the pay package. This would be done to enhance the pension and so make up ground which might otherwise have been lost because of the job change. This is only likely to be the case where someone with very special skills is being sought by a new employer, but it may also be possible in other cases where the employee is willing to take less pay if the employer will enhance his pension. The 'earnings cap' will make matters much more difficult in this respect and as the ceiling is lowered, in real terms, progressively, the problems will affect more and more job changers.

(f) AVCs and FSAVCs

Additional Voluntary Contribution schemes assist an employee with less than a full career before him or her to make up the standard pension entitlement nearer to the maximum. AVCs are explained in detail in Chapter 7.

Free Standing Additional Voluntary Contributions are much the same, except that the contributions are paid to an outside agency rather than to the trustees of the pension fund. It is not a popular concept with pension fund administrators but may be advantageous to use where an employee changes jobs but wishes to continue with an existing policy.

(g) The profitable leaver

It is argued that in a final pay scheme there is a 'profit' made when a member leaves. Suppose the scheme has been set up assuming that

69

income from investments will be, say 9%, and pay increases awarded to members will be, say, 7.5% each year. The results achieved if the actual rates of increase are, respectively, 12% and 10.5%, will not vary by much so long as the differential is constant. But if a member leaves, and so has no pay increase except the 5% LPI to be taken into account, there is a considerable change in the results. In the second example the money representing the value of the deferred pension will indeed make a 'profit' for the pension scheme equal to the difference between the assumed 10.5% and the actual 5% increases in benefit, that is 5.5% p.a.

Much the same argument can be mounted concerning pensioners. While inflation is below 5% these arguments lose face.

(h) The effects of inflation

More generally, on the question of the effects of inflation, it could be the case that members are given the opportunity to take a lower opening pension (say one-eightieth of pay for each year of service instead of one-sixtieth) but to have a built-in escalation at a rate calculated to give the same total return to the member. Unfortunately, experience in these matters tends to show that the bird in the hand is usually preferred, if the matter is left to individual choice.

(i) Personal pensions

It is argued, with some accuracy, that personal or money purchase pensions do not give rise to problems with leavers. Young employees and those in jobs that, almost by definition, will call for job changing if they are to progress, are likely to do better with these schemes, at least in their earlier years. Even then, a bout of severe inflation will deal a heavy blow to their expectations, particularly if it occurs near to retirement.

(j) Hybrid schemes

This has led some consultants to recommend a combination of final pay and money purchase. The trouble about that is that the employer must get the worst of all worlds if the employee gets the best.

Chapter 10

Investment media

1. Insured — to be or not to be

In the smaller occupational pension scheme the selection of an insurance company will be virtually the only investment decision to be made. This will often be decided by the employing company, perhaps even before the trust deed has been sealed. An insurance company can give certain guarantees and it may be important to have these guarantees. It must be remembered however, that there is a price attached to them. The first question to ask is whether there are sufficiently few lives in the scheme to make it almost essential to insure the death risks. It is perfectly practical to have a self-administered scheme but to re-insure the death in service benefits and perhaps widow(er)s' pensions as well. The second question is whether there is sufficient new money coming forward to obtain a reasonable spread of investments. If there is not then it is much better to invest as part of a larger pool of money and an insurance company is the most obvious way of doing this. In fact, for many years, it was the only alternative method to full self-investment. As pension schemes became larger the insurance companies realised that they stood to lose the business of many of them who would decide to become self-administered if that was the only alternative. It was therefore a natural development for insurance companies to offer an arrangement known as a managed fund. A managed fund is a pool of money managed by the insurance company for a number of pension fund clients who do not consider themselves large enough to be self-administered but who do think they are large enough not to require the guarantees which the full insurance policy would bring them. In these circumstances the trustees still have no say over which investments are purchased or sold, but the return on the investment belongs to the trustees according to the proportion of the managed fund which represents their part of it. The insurance company receives, in effect, a management fee for investing the money.

The next development was to go one step further than an overall managed fund and have a separate managed fund, known as a segregated fund, for each particular pension scheme. The trustees still have no direct say over which particular investments are bought or sold but they do have certain assets hypothecated specifically to their scheme and, therefore, they are as near as practical to being a self-administered scheme (without having

71

to be concerned with the selection of securities or the management of the arrangement from the administrative point of view).

Today, many insurance companies will act as the investment manager for what is effectively a self-administered scheme, so that insurance companies can be considered in that respect like any other investment adviser.

It is very difficult to say at what precise size of scheme or perhaps more pertinently, what amount of new money needs to be coming forward, to justify moving from one stage to another of the particular chain I have just described. Clearly, £10,000 a year is too little to invest on its own account and equally clearly, £10,000,000 a year is more than adequate to qualify to be a fully self-administered scheme. Personally, I would think that new money to be invested should reach a level of about £100,000 a year before one would look outside the traditional insurance arrangement. The administrative costs of going self-administered with a capital base of much less than £1m would seem to be disproportionate.

2. Investment advisers

(a) Choices

There are a number of types of investment adviser.

Merchant banks probably have between them the largest amount of money under management.

In addition, most of the joint stock banks have a trustee and executor department who would take on the responsibilities for managing self-administered pension schemes.

Then there are stockbrokers. There are several hundred members of the London Stock Exchange and some of the larger firms have considerable amounts of money under management. There are some strongly held views about whether or not stockbrokers should be employed to operate a self-administered scheme. On the one hand they may charge a lower fee, relying on the commissions generated for their firms by buying and selling the securities. It is however this very point, that they are gaining commission by buying and selling, which leads to the view that maybe the portfolio will be 'churned'. This is a term used to indicate that there may be a greater volume of buying and selling than would otherwise by justified in order to increase the income of the stockbroker. I do not believe this to be the case and there is no evidence to suggest that stockbrokers buy or sell investments except where such transactions are carried out in order to obtain a better return for the client. We shall be discussing performance measurement later in this chapter and I believe that in that measurement there is sufficient protection. It would be a very skilful operator indeed who could obtain an acceptable return for his client and in addition, make unnecessary changes to the portfolio (which themselves are very costly to perform; there is always a 0.5% stamp duty which is levied on all equity purchases for example).

The reorganisation of the Stock Exchange, agreed with the Government to avoid a case being brought by the Office of Fair Trading, the Big Bang of October 1986, makes it more difficult for pension fund administrators to ensure for the trustees the best possible dealing. The OFT case was that the Stock Exchange enjoyed a virtual monopoly, and, because it also stipulated minimum dealing commissions, this was against the public interest. The reorganisation, which has led to the dismantling of the minimum commission structure, also included provisions to allow non-Stock Exchange members to own 100% of broking and jobbing firms and for the dismantling of what is known as 'single capacity'. This was the requirement that a broker and jobber work respectively as agent and principal but that neither work as both — 'dual capacity'. Apart from the opportunity to earn more commission by doing both jobs, it is difficult to see what this has to do with the OFT case.

For the pension fund administrator it causes problems in that he will never again be able to be absolutely sure that when he places a buying order, the broker will get for him the very lowest price. This is because the broker may also be making a market in that security and have a line of that particular stock of which he wishes to dispose (for himself or another client), so clearly he will wish to obtain the highest price. Of course, the argument goes, there must be a declaration if the broker is acting as a market maker and a net price (without commission) is charged. But, by definition, a broker is working for his client and is professionally bound to get the best deal. A market maker is working on his own account and the better he does for his client, the less well he does for himself.

If there were perfect and instant access to the details of all deals then the objection would be lessened, but even then it would be the pension funds who would end up paying for the communication system as they did for the present one and for the Council for the Securities Industry and the Take-Over Panel. The rush to buy into broking and jobbing firms by banks, merchant banks and overseas banks at extraordinary multiples of the historically high earnings of 1983 and 1984 indicated that they expected returns to be equally exceptionally high in the future. This was difficult to square with the objective that the consumer would benefit, which usually means a reduction in costs. Add to that the extraordinary salaries which were being quoted for job changers in the City, and the question had to be asked, who was to pay for all this?

A number of specialist firms have been created especially to look after pension fund monies. Very often the founder of the business was himself an investment manager of a pension fund and this has been a natural development of his skills.

There will also be a number of other houses who have, as their principal business, the investment management of other forms of pooled arrangements like investment trusts or unit trusts and these firms too will see taking on the management of occupational pension arrangements as a natural extension of their business.

There has also been developed, as a service to clients, investment advisory services offered by some firms of actuaries and accountants.

(b) Fees

Apart from stockbrokers, who derive remuneration from the commissions which they charge on sales and purchases of investments, the other advisers generally charge a fixed fee based on the market value of the investments which they are managing. The percentage may be quite high in the case of small funds. In the case of the larger funds, it is probably 0.2% or 0.3%. By using market value there is a certain element of performance reward but the type of incentive payment which is often found in the United States is uncommon in the United Kingdom. This system of reward depending on results may well develop as performance measurement becomes more sophisticated. Performance measurement is dealt with in greater detail later on in this chapter.

(c) Mandate

If investment advisers are appointed, there must be some agreed basis on which they are to act. Although they may be given a very free hand, there must be some point at which the trustees or the asset management company will want to make policy decisions. There should be an investment policy framework letter addressed to the adviser (or advisers) which sets out his responsibilities clearly. It will say how much new money is likely to be coming forward; when it will be available; how dealings are to take place; whether there are to be any general or specific inhibitions or restrictions; how often reports are required; what figures will need to be made available; the administrative details and the fee. This type of contract does not usually include a period of notice on termination because if it is decided, for some reason, to make a change then usually the change takes place immediately. An example of an investment policy framework letter is set out in Appendix 9 (page 125).

The Financial Services Act 1986 introduced the concept of self-regulation to nearly all aspects of selling and giving advice in the financial markets. The Investment Management Regulatory Organisation (IMRO) has been the agency chosen by most investment houses and the NAPF had discussions in the early days to establish rules and procedures for pension funds. The NAPF itself did not seek to become a self-regulatory body.

(d) Employed advisers

Many of the very large schemes go one step further than employing outside advisers, and employ their own investment manager, together with the necessary team. Clearly the fund must be fairly large to justify the overhead which is involved. There will be no real difference between an outside adviser and an employed manager. He must still be given a clear brief of what he is expected to do and he will still be measured on what it is he has done. Very often the investment manager will actually report through a route in the employing company's hierarchy different from that of the manager responsible for the administration of the benefits side of the scheme.

In other cases one or other of these managers will be senior to the other and the reporting will be through a single line. Equally, it will sometimes be the case that an investment manager has a direct responsibility for a property portfolio but in other cases his brief will be confined to Stock Exchange securities.

Clearly any change, for example as a result of poor investment performance, will involve all the notices and payments relevant to a dismissal. There will also be the time and cost of recruiting a replacement. For these reasons, and because of the Financial Services Act, some very large pension funds indeed have decided to put the business out. If they do not, then IMRO registration will be required.

(e) Property advisers

Because property comes in fairly large financial parcels and because it is not as readily marketable as Stock Exchange securities, direct property investment will be confined to the larger funds. For smaller funds there is the pooling arrangement to be found in unit trusts, and a number of these have been set up especially for approved pension schemes. Because of this fact they obtain the same tax advantages as a scheme which invests directly in property. Where there is direct investment in property, chartered surveyors are usually appointed to give an independent valuation upon each sale or purchase. These firms are often used in connection with rent reviews and with valuation of the property portfolio for the actuary's used. Unless the portfolio is very large indeed, the day-to-day management of the properties will also be looked after by an outside firm of chartered surveyors. The activities under this heading could cover the collection of rents, making sure that each tenant observes his covenants (for example, there may be a requirement to paint the interior at certain intervals) and in various ways improving the quality of the investment so that a higher return can be obtained.

The costs involved in having a property portfolio will be rather higher than for a Stock Exchange portfolio but on the other hand properties will not be dealt in as frequently.

(f) Cash management

The next area which we must look at is the question of cash. Particularly in times of high interest rates, the day-to-day management of cash will be a very important part of the overall return obtained for a pension scheme. The money market is as near perfect as any of the markets that can be found and apart from odd times during the year, such as when income tax becomes payable or certain settlements become due, there will be little point in shopping around for better rates. The investment advisers may be charged with the task of investing cash not required for immediate investment through the money market, or this can be done direct through money brokers.

It is interesting to note that the money handling charges which most joint stock banks charge will normally be waived if the bank's own money market division is used. If the rates of that bank's money market division are the same as those available elsewhere, therefore, it will be an advantage to invest with them.

3. Overseas investments

A topic which will be dealt with more fully in Chapter 14 concerns the rights and wrongs of investing money overseas. Leaving that question aside for the purpose of this chapter, the investment advisers or the investment manager would normally embrace within the Stock Exchange portfolio an overseas element, if there is to be one. Once again, smaller funds will not be able to put together sufficient monies in overseas investment to obtain a reasonably balanced portfolio. This could well result in the purchase of some specialist unit trusts to obtain holdings of US securities or Japanese stocks or whatever market it is in which the trustees seek representation. This does raise a rather interesting question: where an adviser also manages a unit trust, should he be discouraged or dissuaded from putting part of the portfolio at his disposal into that trust? On the one hand he would be expected to know more about that trust than any other and presumably would wish to invest in it only if he felt that the returns were going to be better than could be obtained elsewhere. On the other hand, if at any time it was desired to change the investment adviser, then it would almost certainly lead to there being a realisation of this security at perhaps not the best time possible. Larger funds may employ specialist advisers for particular overseas markets or give particular brokers a brief to obtain a portfolio in the Pacific basin or Australia or North America or Europe.

4. Performance measurement

(a) Stock Exchange portfolio

Performance measurement is a relatively recent development and to an extent, the process is still going on to develop a better overall system of comparing the performance of a particular pension fund with that of other investors or with the market generally, or against some index which gives an indication of whether good progress is being made or otherwise.

The easiest part of the portfolio to measure is the Stock Exchange portfolio. This is because there is a Stock Exchange daily list which quotes the prices of all stocks and shares and from this a middle market price (mid way between the quoted selling and buying price) is established each day for practically every 'quoted' security. Of course, some securities are dealt in more frequently than others. It would be unusual for a pension fund to invest heavily in those sectors of the market which are regarded as either infrequently dealt in or downright unmarketable. For many years now the *Financial Times* has run a number of indices, which are described more fully in Chapter 11.

With these indices readily available, it is fairly easy to obtain a crude reference to see how your own portfolio has performed against one or other or several of the indices. In order to iron out differences, because of the amount of money coming forward to the particular portfolio under review and the time that it comes forward, there are processes known as time weighting and money weighting which provide rather more sophisticated indicators.

Since the early 1970s most of the larger firms of actuaries have set up performance measurement services comparing the investment results of their own clients, and indeed anyone else who wished to take part in those services (see page 82).

(b) Property

Until very recently a property portfolio was difficult indeed to measure from the performance point of view. Of course it was possible to say what the rents represented in terms of an income return. Increases in capital value could be established from time to time although that itself is an expensive exercise. A system based on what is known as the internal rate of return has been developed and has been used by individual pension schemes for some time. There are also firms of chartered surveyors who offer property performance measurement services.

5. Other securities

Allowance has to be made for any securities in an overseas portfolio and for cash to establish an overall return for the pension scheme.

I have not dealt at all with such matters as investment in commodities or works of art or postage stamps, because for pension schemes which do not have to pay income tax, it is generally regarded as being better to invest in securities which have an income flow. For those schemes which do venture into these specialist areas, there will have to be suitable advice available and to the cost of this advice there will very often have to be added other costs such as insurance or storage which themselves will have to be taken into account in arriving at a return on the original investment.

Another specialist area will be venture capital. This is where the pension scheme will put money into very small or new businesses. Experience here is that the selection and control of such investments is very costly in terms of management time. Unless a reasonable spread of such opportunities can be undertaken the ratio of the rewards against the risk will be insufficiently high. It is also evident that if only 1% of the fund is to be risked in this way, even fantastically good returns are not going to make a significant difference to the overall return.

If there were a road sign which could be commended to trustees it would probably read — 'Caution — Investment decisions ahead'.

Chapter 11

Investment choices

1. The Stock Exchange

(a) General

The first type of investment which most people think about is one made through the Stock Exchange.

Many will be familiar with the origins of the Stock Exchange. When, in the eighteenth century, undertakings became too large or too risky for one individual, and at that time we were normally talking about a maritime adventure, a group of 'investors' would get together to share the risks and the rewards. Let us say that they wished to bring back tea from India; this would be a highly speculative investment but one offering very high returns. Maybe twenty or thirty merchants would come together to finance the operation. The time period over which the money would be tied up before the return of capital could be made and a profit realised might be several months or even years. During that prolonged period there could well be situations arising where one or more of the original investors needed to settle other debts or where they saw what they believed to be better opportunities to invest their money. Initially such investors would go round the coffee houses in the City of London, literally calling out their wish to sell an interest in an adventure. When a possible buyer came forward it would then be a question of determining how much the share was worth and, if the two parties could agree, there would be an exchange of interest.

With the Industrial Revolution in the nineteenth century the capital required to build and equip factories, develop mines or quarries, indeed to finance the very extensive house building programmes in the emerging towns, produced a requirement which was not only greater than that of the merchant venturers but was required for a much longer term. Gradually different sorts of lenders and borrowers were matched. For example, the industrialist who wished to build a factory might require £20,000. He may have calculated that the profits from the manufacturing which would take place in that building would allow him to pay the current rate of interest, which may have been 3%, leaving him with a profit.

This profit might be more than sufficient to provide the necessary resources to keep his factory going. There might be a surplus which would enable him to put aside enough money each year to be able to repay the initial borrowing over a period of, say, twenty years. He would thus arrange to borrow the money, with the security of the building underlying it, at an interest rate of 3% each year. In addition, he would guarantee to repay the loan at the end of the twenty-year period. This is the present day fixed interest redeemable security, maybe a debenture or an unsecured loan stock. Alternatively, it may be that a very great deal more money was required. For example, to acquire sufficient land to sink mines and to bring up coal — it would be very difficult to establish at the beginning what sort of annual return could be paid, let alone whether a staged repayment of the capital was possible.

This type of situation lent itself very much more to a grouping of individuals who would put an amount in, rather like the original merchant venturers and who would share whatever profits emerged. However, unlike the maritime adventure, there would be no specific time-scale. Therefore these shares were issued with no guaranteed rate of annual income and no guaranteed repayment date. This is the present day ordinary share, sometimes referred to as the equity.

Between these two extremes of borrowing there could be a hundred and one different variations.

Having created an adventure or company, it very soon became equally important to have an opportunity to establish an exchange or market for those who for one reason or another wished to come out of that particular investment. They would then be able to sell to those who might wish to come into such an investment but who perhaps did not have money available at the time that the new issue was being made.

(b) Dealing

The Stock Exchange grew from these beginnings to become the leading financial market in securities, bringing together borrowers and lenders. Nowadays it is not necessary for the owner of a particular stock or share to walk around the City of London coffee houses seeking a buyer.

The market is a highly sophisticated affair. It used to comprise jobbers on the 'floor' of the Stock Exchange, who would quote a buying and selling price for any of the shares quoted on the Exchange. Brokers, on behalf of their clients, would approach the jobbers with orders to buy and sell certain securities. Normally the broker was given a price or range of prices by his client. There was a minimum commission (often erroneously called a fixed commission) payable by the client. The position now is that there are market makers who act as principals, that is on their own account, who make deals at net prices. It is still possible to appoint your own agent who will work on your behalf and will charge a negotiated commission. Every working day many thousands of transactions take place. When you deal in Government securities settlement will be made the next day. With other securities dealings are for an account, which is normally a two-week period. The purchase of an interest, whether it be a debenture, an unsecured loan stock, a preference or ordinary share, will be evidenced by a document issued by the company concerned. This evidence is, of course, forthcoming only upon the registration of the new owner. The more immediate paperwork is a contract note from the broker setting out the name and type of security purchased or sold, the cost or the sale proceeds and such other matters as the broker's commission, stamp duty and so on.

Although the 'floor' is now a VDU and what used to be a physical approach is now a telephone contact, the idea is exactly the same.

The other 'markets' — Commodities Markets and LIFFE (the London International Financial Futures Exchange) should also be mentioned. Then there are the overseas Bourses of Europe, Wall Street in New York, and the Tokyo Exchange.

After many delays and a considerable investment in a system called TAURUS a different sort of 'paperless' transactions system is to be introduced and, gradually, starting with the larger companies, certificates of ownership will give way to computer records. The evidence of ownership will be the broker's note that a security has been purchased and registered on your behalf. It is also intended to introduce a rolling settlement system to replace the present system of account dealing.

(c) The Stock Exchange zoo

A curious collection of animals seems to inhabit the Stock Exchange from time to time. They may be explained as follows:

A *bull* is an investor who believes that prices on the Stock Exchange generally, or of a particular security or type of security in which he is investing are likely to do well.

A *bear*, on the other hand, takes the opposite point of view and is generally a seller.

A *stag* is an investor who takes a bullish view of a new issue and is prepared to borrow money in order to apply for more shares than he actually wants. He does this in the hope that he will be able to sell any shares allotted to him immediately after the issue, to realise an immediate profit. He is thereby able to repay the loan leaving himself with the difference as a profit.

(d) The FT Index and others

Because not all the companies whose shares make up the index are the same size an allowance is made in assessing each company's shares as a percentage of the total market. This is called 'weighting'. In order to express, in brief terms, how the market has moved generally there are various groupings of securities which are valued on a 'weighted' basis to give an overall impression of that area of Stock Exchange activity. Perhaps the most well-known index is the *FT Index* of thirty ordinary shares. Although this is only a tiny fraction of the number of shares quoted on the London Stock Exchange, they are believed to be indicative of the market as a whole and very rapid calculations can be made to show whether, on a particular day, the market generally has done well or badly. There are of course very many other indices. The *FT All Share Index* has a total of 750 shares and for a pension fund gives perhaps a more reliable indicator of how the market is behaving. There are also indices of various gilt-edged (government) securities and other types of stock.

There are various other bench-marks which enable investors to judge how well they have fared compared with others. For example, for pensions funds there are two large measurement services, the WM (or World Markets, formerly Wood McKenzie) and CAPS (or Combined Actuaries Performance Service), which record the progress of large numbers of funds and arrive at a league table subdivided into funds of similar sizes.

(e) Indexed funds

The idea of assessing performance by reference to one or more indices has been taken further over the last few years. Some advisers now offer to invest in line with one index or other, and guarantee to produce a return which exactly reflects the index chosen, subject only to a narrowly defined allowance for variation.

2. Unquoted securities

Then there are unquoted securities. These are shares in private companies or businesses which are not quoted on the London Stock Exchange or a foreign Exchange. While there are some very large private companies, in general one tends to think of a private company as being somewhat smaller than a public company, possibly offering greater growth opportunities. It is natural to associate a greater potential with a greater risk, and generally pension funds do not invest a great deal in private companies. Those pension funds which do, tend to think of the investment as a special situation which needs particular initial investigation and continuing watchful care. One of the reasons for this is that there is no market, so that if such an investment is judged not to be doing very well, the chances of selling it quickly are virtually nil.

There are other special situations which arise on the initiative of the pension fund itself. For example, it may form a private company in order to carry out a particular project, joining with other pension funds or other investors to spread its risk.

Quite a lot of publicity was attracted a few years ago, when one or two pension funds entered into dealings in the commodities market and in the fine arts field. Generally speaking, the view is taken that a tax-free pension fund is best advised to concentrate on those investments which produce income. Particularly at times of very high rates of interest, the resources of the fund will accumulate very quickly. A non-income bearing security will need to show considerable capital gains on sale to keep pace.

3. Property

There is, however, one unquoted security which most large pension funds will regard as a suitable part of their portfolio. I refer, of course, to direct investment in property. Property has the advantage of having an income from rents and capital appreciation as the value of the underlying buildings increases. This appreciation is likely to be at least in line with inflation because new buildings will cost more to construct. Obviously this point is only valid so long as the building is where tenants wish to be — hence the saying that there are three important points about selecting properties: (i) location (ii) location and (iii) location! There is also protection in that it should be possible to attract an alternative tenant if one particular tenant should fail for any reason. The record of the performance of property over the last twenty years or so has been good and compares favourably with Stock Exchange securities. Short-term measurement is not likely to be suitable for this type of investment. Periods like 1974−1975 and 1990−1992 have shown that the class of security is not a one-way bet, but the short-term investor risks buying at the top and/or selling at the bottom of the cycle — either or both of which will produce a particularly unsatisfactory return.

As with all types of security there are different classes of property investment. Freehold properties or very long leaseholds are favoured by pension funds because they fit in well with long-term liabilities. (Short leaseholds will be more attractive to certain types of private investor who may be able to obtain tax advantages.) Generally portfolios are divided up into office buildings; shop premises; and commercial or industrial buildings. The last group will give the highest income returns but have less potential capital growth. Shops have lower initial returns but have an excellent record of capital appreciation.

Tenants are now usually offered leases of twenty to twenty-five years with the rent to be reviewed (upwards only) every five years to the then market value. Pension funds prefer to offer leases where the tenant is responsible for all the expenses of running the building, including insurance.

Inevitably there is some management involved, if only to collect rents (normally quarterly) and make sure that the tenant is sticking to the terms of his lease. For example, it may be a condition that the interior is painted every five years, or that a car parking area is kept in good repair.

Somebody must carry out these checks. If the pension fund does not have its own staff to do this, there are many firms of chartered surveyors who may be retained for a fee. Even where there are staff in-house, trustees will usually obtain independent property valuations at purchase, upon sale and at, say, three yearly intervals.

4. Overseas investment

There has been a great deal of comment about investment overseas, especially since exchange control regulations were lifted towards the end of 1979. The arguments against range from the motive — 'taking away jobs from the United Kingdom' — to the practical problems of currency risks. The counter arguments are that overseas investment offers greater spread of risk and the opportunity to put money into ventures not possible in the UK. These used to include utilities (although gas, water and electricity are now very much available in the UK), robotics and the silicon 'chip'. Not many funds will have put more than 20% or so of their money overseas and even then the geographical spread may cover the USA, Europe, the Far East and Australia. Investments may range from bio-technology to electric power companies, from uranium mines to software houses. The known additional risks will be taken only where there is an expectation of an above average return.

A few years ago, many of the larger pension funds took a position in US real estate. Smaller funds were able to make a similar move through unit trusts. The attraction was that the real estate market in the US had never found favour with the institutions there who preferred to offer mortgages. More recently, the fashion has been to look to the newly emerging markets of the Pacific Rim and Latin America. Naturally, only a small percentage of the fund would be placed in these markets.

5. Distribution of assets between markets

Apart from not putting all the eggs in one basket, what ground rules will the trustees of an occupational pension fund adopt? Certainly they will go for a spread of investments. Larger funds tend to have 55 – 70% in equities quoted on the London Stock Exchange, perhaps 15 – 25% overseas and, maybe 10% in property.

Property may be further subdivided, quite possibly equally between offices, shops, and commercial buildings. The fund may select four or five regions throughout the UK and concentrate on these. In this way the areas can be researched in a more detailed way. Management will also be easier. Usually only the best positions are sought, namely prime properties. This tends to mean a lower opening income yield. Pension funds have to show performance over a very long period, however, and short-term advantage is seldom the objective.

Stock Exchange securities will also show a spread. This may be 80% equities (ordinary shares) and 20% gilts (government securities). Equities will be further subdivided into sectors – electrical, stores, engineering, oils — and each sector will have a characteristic income and capital growth pattern.

6. Income yield

Perhaps it would be as well to explain how income yield is obtained. If an ordinary share costs 80p and the total paid in a year by way of dividend is 4p the yield is 4 divided by 80. This is usually expressed as a percentage, in this case 5%. Gilts offer a higher income return but, apart from the recently issued index-linked gilts, there is no prospect of income growth. Index-linked gilts are more like equities, but with an even lower initial income yield. Income will, however, keep pace with price inflation and at a fixed future date each £100 invested will be repaid to reflect price inflation also. If prices have doubled during the life of the stock the repayment will be £200 for each £100 invested.

7. Valuation

So how do the trustees know if they are doing well or badly? It is relatively easy to value Stock Exchange securities. There is a daily list of all deals from which a middle market price is established. Although you could neither buy nor sell at this price it is a reasonable indication. All the larger companies' shares, often called 'blue chips', are traded actively and the 'spread' (the difference between buying and selling price) is quite small. For example, 53–54, 96–98, 242–246. Gilt-edge securities are sold in £100 nominal units and here prices may be 92.25–92.75. (It must be remembered that buying and selling costs have to be taken into account when a deal is done.) Probably each month the whole Stock Exchange portfolio of the pension fund is valued. Certainly at the year-end there will be a valuation, and book value and market value will probably both be shown in the accounts.

Property is not the subject of active trading and so valuations are likely to be undertaken only infrequently. Because it is a costly procedure it is likely to be commissioned every three years, with one-third of the properties being valued every third year so that a smoother trend is established.

Overseas securities will normally be quoted on Wall Street, the Tokyo Exchange or the appropriate national Stock Exchange.

Perhaps the greatest test is whether your fund has matched the consulting actuary's predictions. This is a very stern test indeed because failure to reach these expectations will mean that the contribution rate will have to be increased or the benefit level will be threatened.

It cannot be emphasised too often that a good investment return, measured by income and capital growth, is absolutely vital to the well-being of any occupational pension scheme.

Chapter 12

Information

1. The Social Security Act 1985

There has from time to time been criticism in the press and from certain trade unions that insufficient information is given to members of pension schemes about how their schemes operate and about the members' own positions in particular. The Goode Committee was also asked to consider this question, but its Report, published towards the end of 1993, found no glaring deficiencies.

The Social Security Act 1985 provides that the 'Social Security Pensions Act 1975 shall be amended in accordance with Schedule 2 to this Act in relation to information about occupational pension schemes'. Schedule 2 gives the Secretary of State power to make Regulations so that information about a scheme's constitution, administration and finances, rights and obligations that arise under it and any other relevant matters must be given to members and prospective members; their spouses and any other qualifying person; and recognised trade unions — Regulations specify which information is to be given in any case and that which may be requested.

It has been stated, as the Government's intention, that the information should enable a pensions expert to analyse a scheme. This ambition appears to me to be exactly what it should not be. Having been involved in the take-over of perhaps 500 or more pension schemes the information available, however sketchy in the eyes of the members or the press, has been sufficient to enable me as a pensions manager to manage it, incorporate it or amend it as required. Information to members should enable *members* to understand it.

Although the Act requires extensive information to be given, most pension funds already did so before the statutory requirement was introduced, in November 1986. Experience shows that once a minimum requirement is set down, that becomes the maximum. It is the quality of the information and its presentation, rather than quantity, which is important.

2. The NAPF Code of Practice

In May 1980, the National Association of Pension Funds, after considerable deliberation among members at conferences and through correspondence, adopted a Code of Practice entitled *Information to members of Pension Schemes.* This Code of Practice has the support of the Association of Consulting Actuaries, the Associated Scottish Life Offices, the Life Offices Association and the Society of Pension Consultants. In a foreword, the then Secretary of State for Social Services, included the words 'I warmly commend all those who have contributed to the drafting of the Code of Practice. They have made a notable contribution to satisfying "the right to know".'

Each chapter is classified under three headings and printed in different coloured type. First, there are the statutory or quasi-legal requirements which are printed in red.

There then follows any further information which schemes ought to give as a minimum requirement. This represents the standard to which the Association commends all pension schemes. This is printed in blue.

Then in green, there is set out a statement of current practice beyond the minimum stated earlier, which may be considered better practice and which is offered as a useful check list for consideration by pension schemes which already satisfy the minimum standards.

After setting out the background to the position as we find it today, the following chapters go into detail under the three headings mentioned earlier.

While not attempting to include in this book complete details of the Code, which itself is eighteen pages long, this is such an important and topical matter that greater detail than might otherwise be given is shown.

(a) Information on entry

Chapter 1 deals with the provision of information — first, that which should be given to an employee on entry to employment; and secondly, on entry to the pensions scheme (other than by a merger of companies; this is dealt with in a later chapter). It is pointed out that the Employment Protection (Consolidation) Act 1978 provides that the employer must give to each new employee within thirteen weeks of starting employment a statement of the main terms of the contract of employment. Among other things, this must contain particulars of any terms and conditions relating to pensions and pension schemes. In addition, the statement must contain a note as to whether a contracting-out certificate under the Social Security Pensions Act 1975 applies. The Code then goes on to say that it is desirable that the provisions of the scheme as set out in a members' handbook should be given to the individual even though entry to the scheme may be later.

Then, under the practice beyond the minimum requirements, there is a suggestion that the question of any transfer values should be discussed with the employee, and any interim life cover which may apply mentioned. It could also be that an outline of the pension scheme was given in an induction course.

On entry to the scheme, the Pension Schemes Office requires certain details to be conveyed to the employee; these are set out in Appendix 1 to the Code. It is also considered desirable to draw attention to any additional options which the employee may exercise at entry, and any voluntary contribution facility. The question of a transfer value coming in, or whether a transfer value can be paid should he later leave the scheme should also be dealt with in some detail. There is then the suggestion that the discretionary provisions concerning death benefits should be described and the member invited to lodge a 'wish letter'. (This has already been dealt with in some detail in Chapter 8.)

It is also considered that the management's power to alter or discontinue the scheme should be explained, as should the tax treatment of employees' contributions. A little detail about the legal position of the member in relation to the trust deed and rules is also recommended. An important point is to state where a copy of these documents can be seen.

When it comes to the practice beyond the minimum, there is a suggestion that up-to-date methods of communication, such as audio-visual presentations, should be used; and that where any options need to be exercised at entry to the scheme, adequate information should be provided to enable the member to make his choice properly.

It is also suggested that the member should be given broad details of the State pension arrangements, if necessary by reference to the relevant leaflets issued by the DSS.

(b) Information on termination or death

Chapter 2 deals with the provision of information to the member on termination of membership, or to the member's family upon his death. There are no specific statutory requirements relating to death benefits, but it is considered that the person dealing with the member's estate, or the possible beneficiaries within the trustees' discretionary powers, should be advised of the benefits which arise as a result of the member's death and should be given details of any options which may exist and told of the conditions governing payment of benefits and the tax position.

As far as practice beyond the minimum is concerned, there is a suggestion that financial advice might be provided, or at least that the sources of such financial advice be pointed out to the dependants, so that any lump sum may be used to the best advantage.

When a member retires it is considered reasonable that some time in advance he should have been given a statement showing the pension payment with any provision for increase, either on a guaranteed or an *ad hoc* basis; the contingent widow's or other dependant's pension which might be payable; any options, including the possibility of converting some of the pension into a lump sum; the frequency and method of pension payment; where further information can be obtained; the system of taxation of the benefits; and details of the interaction between the State pension and occupational pension scheme.

Practice beyond the minimum is much the same as that described under death of a member.

Where a member leaves service before retirement, it is considered right that he should be given much the same details about his immediate pension. In addition there should be a note about how the deferred pensioner should claim his pension and how the trustees will attempt to trace him.

(c) Periodic information

Chapter 3 deals with periodic information to members. It is considered prudent, although perhaps not strictly a statutory requirement, that as much information as is practicable should be available to members. This would include the right to inspect, on request, the trust deed and rules; the audited accounts; actuarial valuation reports; and general information about investments or insurance contracts which may affect the benefits.

Under desirable further information, it is considered that, on request, a formal annual trustees' report should be made available which would contain the audited accounts; details of the investments (pointing out any investment which involves the employing company or matters of that sort); a statement prepared by the actuary; including his most recent recommendations concerning contributions and whether or not these contributions have been paid.

Under the general heading of personal information, it is considered that there should be the possibility of a periodic personal benefits statement giving details of the individual's benefits. There should be encouragement to advise the administrator of changes in personal circumstances, such as marriage or changes of dependants in one way or another. Under practice beyond the minimum, it is suggested that there should be an annual personal statement given to every current active member, in which all or some of the following details should be given:

- benefits payable at normal retirement with any options available;
- death in service benefits, including possible beneficiaries;
- death after retirement benefits, giving details similar to those for death in service benefits;
- leaving service, details of deferred pensions and any options which are available as far as the transfers are concerned;
- pensions increases, statement of any guaranteed increase or the policy of reviewing on a regular basis; and
- notes giving any further information which may be thought to

be helpful (which might include a note of the changes in Lower and Upper Earnings Limits).

(d) Information on mergers etc

Chapter 4 deals with the provision of information on the merger of companies or on the structural change of a scheme. This matter is dealt with fully in Chapter 3 of this book.

3. Training

(a) Courses

What about courses for newly appointed trustees? Since 1972 the NAPF jointly with the Industrial Society has run a three-day trusteeship course which has been extremely well received. Briefly, the course covers:

- Pension scheme design — background information about pension scheme planning and design.
- Legal responsibilities of pension fund trustees — what the law requires of trustees.
- The members' voice — what is the responsibility of the trustees to the members? Is there a special role for an employees' representative?
- Pension Schemes — funding — How pensions are funded; surpluses and deficiencies — to whom do they belong and what should be done about them? Pension fund accounting.
- Exercising discretionary powers — disposal of death benefits under pension funds, augmenting pensions at retirement etc.
- Meetings of trustees — delegates break into small groups to consider typical problems which might confront trustees.
- Information for the employee — what does the employee need to know? How should the information be supplied to him? What is the purpose of effective communication?
- Running a pension scheme — its legal constitution, documentation and recording. Approval by statutory bodies. Administrative systems. Contracting-out procedures.
- Investment policy — the trustee's role — how should trustees control the investment policy of a pension fund and to what extent should they delegate responsibility for day to day decisions.

The General Municipal and Boilermakers Union and the Transport and General Workers Union also run courses for their own members; these too have been well received and are highly commended.

There are several courses arranged by commercial undertakings but it should not be thought that these are intended merely as exercises to sell consultancy services to delegates. The fact is that certain consultants have been asked by their clients to help in this direction; this had led to their setting up seminars which eventually have become open to the public generally. My brother and I run such courses and we go further, where required, and supply independent trustees for clients.

(b) Literature

To complement the joint NAPF/Industrial Society course is a boxed set of booklets (A5 size) published by the NAPF, and written by well-known practitioners who are experts in their particular subjects. The series would be invaluable to all those concerned with pension trusteeship. The aspects covered are:

- legal
- actuarial
- secretarial
- discretionary powers
- reports and accounts
- investments.

This is a useful permanent reference for newly appointed trustees.

4. Benefit statements

The 1985 Act covers the general subject of information, or 'disclosure' as it is rather mischievously called. Regulations brought the Act into force for each scheme year which commences after 1 November 1986.

Members have the right, upon request, to be given a benefit statement annually. Most administrators decided to issue benefit statements automatically each year to all members. As one would expect, the statement should give details of:

- retirement benefit; and
- death benefit.

The annual amounts should be quoted. It is the early leaver benefits which will give most problems. In these cases it is necessary to quote the:

- transfer value on leaving;
- value of deferred benefits; and
- value of refund of contributions.

The latter is applicable only to those with less than two years' membership. This causes an enormous amount of work, most of which is totally unproductive.

The statement will, naturally, have to show where further information may be obtained or queries addressed.

5. Annual reports

The 1985 Act also contains provision for annual reports. As with personal benefit statements the report is to be available on request, but most administrators will decide to make an automatic issue. Recognised trade unions are also entitled to receive a copy. The employer must inform new employees of the basic details of the scheme:

- eligibility options;
- which employments are included;
- how benefits are calculated;
- contributions payable by members and employers;
- the basis on which pensions in payment are price protected;
- the rights of early leavers;

and, again, where further information can be obtained.

Then, each year, a report must give, as a minimum:

- trustees' and advisers' names and contact points;
- members' and trade union rights;
- any amendments made during the year;
- the number of members and pensioners with changes during the year;
- details of pension increases;
- details of transfer values paid out and accepted in;
- confirmation that contributions have been paid;
- details of the scheme finances;
- details of investments including management and performance;
- audited accounts; and
- a statement by the actuary.

My personal experience of giving information to members, ranging from a single sheet to a 32-page booklet, rather indicates that whatever is done will fail to satisfy some of the members. Some will criticise a long report as too wordy and difficult to read; others will criticise a short report as too sketchy. It is extremely difficult to judge precisely what is the right information to give.

The National Association of Pension Funds started a competition in 1980 called the 'Golden Pen' award for the best annual report to members. It was necessary to break this into two classes so that there should not be a comparison between a formal report and a more popular edition of that information. In fact, a third class was also instituted to cover smaller schemes.

6. Information about scheme documents

The Trust Deed and rules together with amending deeds and a schedule of the names and addresses of all participating companies must be available for inspection by any member, prospective member, prospective beneficiary or recognised trade union. A reasonable charge may be made if copies of documents are requested by any of the parties entitled to inspect them.

7. Further reading

There is a list of publications of the National Association of Pension Funds, 12−18 Grosvenor Gardens, London SW1W 0DH; telephone (071) 730 0585, at the end of this book; see pages 127−128.

In addition, the Pensions Management Institute, PMI House, 4−10 Artillery Lane, London E1 7LS; telephone (071) 247 1452, publish material for those taking professional examinations and, in particular, have published jointly with the Pensions Research Accountants Group, a Glossary of Terms, mentioned earlier.

Besides *Pensions World*, which has been published for many years, there are a number of pension periodicals now available. Some, like *Pensions* and *Pensions Intelligence*, are commercially produced, while others are produced by consultants for their clients and prospective clients.

Chapter 13

The Pension Law Review Committee Report

The Committee was set up in July 1992, under the chairmanship of Professor Roy Goode, on the recommendation of the House of Commons Select Committee on Social Security which had examined the Maxwell affair. Its Report (Cm 2342−I) and the Research Paper (Cm 2342−II) was published on 30 September 1993. The two volumes are priced at £71.30.

The Committee studied 1,669 pieces of written evidence, held public meetings and took oral evidence. It commissioned the research set out in Volume II and visited the United States, Canada, Australia, Brussels and Dublin.

Five dominant issues were revealed by the responses:

  (i)   Surpluses;

  (ii) Trustees;

  (iii) Information;

  (iv) Balance of power; and

  (v)   Security of pensions.

Certain basic criteria were identified leading to six key proposals:

  (a) Trust Law should continue as the foundation for pension funds, but it should be reinforced by a Pensions Act administered by a pensions regulator.

  (b) Freedom of trust should be limited in order to protect accrued rights and to allow members to make their own appointments to the trustee body.

  (c) Provision of information should be improved both in content and in clarity and presentation.

  (d) Security of benefits should be strengthened by the introduction of minimum solvency requirements and a compensation scheme should be established.

  (e) Employers should otherwise be free to amend or terminate their schemes in respect of future benefits.

  (f) Administrative burdens should be reduced, flexibility increased and the law simplified. In particular, a general prudent person standard should replace detailed statutory investment rules and a single tax system based on the 1989 regime adopted.

There are 218 recommendations, none of which could be described as revolutionary. There was no view taken on taxation limitations. Small schemes, those with less than fifty active members and pensioners, should, it was suggested, be subject to some special treatment.

The more important points are summarised below using the reference number, where appropriate, in the Report. (My comments are in brackets.)

1. An Occupational Pensions Scheme Act should lay out a properly structured framework to be regulated by a pensions regulator. (This is bound to involve more legislation and regulation which means costs.)

2. Trust Law should be retained but some modifications are required. (Every pensions lawyer will have a different view.)

3. Some shift in the distribution of power between employers and trustees is necessary. (This is dealt with by suggestions that members should elect or select a number of trustees.)

7. Trust Law should be amended to protect accrued rights (many Trust Deeds already do this).

10. The primary duties of trustees in relation to the pension promise should be set out in legislation. (This may cause conflicts with Trust Law and, in particular, the exercise of discretions.)

There are a number of detailed proposals relating to 'surpluses' and, in particular, that:

15. No 'contribution holiday' should be permitted if as a result the solvency level fell below 100%.

16. The five-year period to eliminate excess over-funding should be extended to the average length of future service up to fifteen years. (This could be in line with Accounting Standard SSAP 24.)

18. Surplus on winding up should continue to be dealt with under the scheme rules. (The problems arise when these rules are not clear or are non-existent. The Report does recognise this point.)

Funding also attracted a number of proposals:

20. A minimum solvency requirement should be necessary for all funded schemes.

22. A solvency band between 90% and 100% should be maintained with an immediate cash injection to be required by the employer within three months where the base level was not maintained (see 29. below).

28. The Government to consider a new type of security to provide more appropriate backing for a scheme's indexed liabilities.

29. A five-year transitional period should be allowed for existing schemes to achieve appropriate standards.

32. Actuarial valuations at intervals of no more than three and a half years do not address the needs. At least an annual statement should be required. (Many actuaries already advocate this course.)

There was much speculation that the Committee would recommend that it should be a requirement to appoint independent trustees, but this is not a feature of the Report. Trustee matters are considered, however, in a number of ways:

34. Disqualification of trustees should be on a similar basis to that of company directors.

35. The actuary and auditor of the scheme should not be permitted to be trustees and good practice should also preclude the administrator.

36. Employers should not have sole powers of appointment.

37. Although there should be no requirement, pensioner trustees should be included in the trustee body. (This is very difficult to organise and generally a pensioner known to be interested in trustee matters is invited to become a trustee.)

38. Earnings related (final pay) schemes' members should have the power to appoint one-third of the trustee body with a minimum of two. (Ever since 1964, when there was a White Paper on the matter, the practice has grown on a voluntary basis.)

39. Money purchase schemes' members should have the power to appoint two-thirds of the trustee body. (This is fair because in these schemes the members take the investment risk.)

41. Scheme members should be free to appoint a non-member or independent trustee.

44. There should be no fixed terms of office for trustees prescribed by law.

45. Employers would have no power to remove a member-appointed trustee.

46. Trustees should be required to:

    ● appoint the auditor, actuary, fund manager and professional advisers;
    ● decide the investment strategy, with the employer;
    ● decide on the distribution of surplus on winding up (This could make an employer uneasy); and
    ● direct the actuary on transfer value principles.

49. Trustees should meet as required to transact business but at

least once a year. Active member trustees should be allowed paid time off to attend meetings and reimbursed reasonable expenses.

52. Employers should be required to allow member trustees reasonable time off for training without loss of pay.

(The question of payment of independent trustees or payment for member trustee training has not been covered.)

Amendment and winding up is given attention.

55. Amendments which prejudice past service benefits should not be permitted.

56. Employers should continue to be allowed to make amendments affecting future service.

64. On insolvency the regulator should have power to appoint a suitable trustee.

Early leavers are dealt with.

69. Limited Price Indexation (LPI), that is escalation in line with increases in the Retail Prices Index with a 5% cap, should continue.

71. Employers should not be allowed to grant enhanced early retirement benefits while not allowing the actuary to make similar allowances in his transfer value calculations.

80. It would not be practical to extend the Transfer of Undertakings (Protection of Employment) Regulations 1981 to cover pension rights.

Administration is given wide consideration.

82. Every scheme should have an actuary appointed by the trustees.

83. The actuary should certify the scheme solvency annually.

84. The trustees have a statutory duty to furnish the actuary with the requisite information and employers should have a corresponding duty to the trustees.

85. The actuary should have a duty to report irregularities to the regulator.

86. The auditor should be appointed by the trustees.

87. The auditor should have a duty to report irregularities to the regulator.

88. Fund managers should be made aware for whom they are acting and from whom to take instructions.

90. The legal adviser's role and terms of reference should be set out formally.

91 – These recommendations deal with time limits for payment over
94 to the trustees of contributions, generally one or two months.

97. Trustees should disclose payments overdue by more than three months.

98. In cases of insolvency the priority given to employers' contributions in respect of GMPs should be extended to all contributions made in the previous twelve months.

99. All schemes should keep separate bank accounts.

Fund management was one of the main areas of study.

104. Flexible guidelines for investment should be adopted in the Pensions Act to replace the Trustee Investments Act 1961 and the Money Purchase Contracted-Out Schemes Regulations 1987.

106. Stock lending, subject to control standards, should continue to be allowed.

107. No changes have been recommended on ethical and socially responsible investment.

108. In-house fund management should be allowed to continue.

Asset safeguards included consideration of an independent custodian but it was not made a requirement.

110. The 5% limit on self investment should stand except that all loans and guarantees to the employer should be prohibited.

111. A five-year disinvestment period of employer related investments above the 5% limit should be allowed and at the end of that period all self-investment, including property, should be brought within the limits.

Insolvency of the employer was another area of concern.

117. Where a scheme is in deficit the employer must make it good.

118. Such a shortfall should not be given priority in the event of insolvency.

120. A compensation scheme should be established but only to deal with losses post the event.

121. The compensation scheme should be limited to loss resulting from fraud, theft or other misappropriation.

125. An independent pension compensation board should be established.

129. There should be no limit on the amount of compensation except that it should not exceed the lesser of 90% of the value of assets misappropriated or 90% of the scheme deficit.

131. The costs of compensation should be shared by all schemes rather than the taxpayer.

Information to scheme members was regarded as vital.

136. Schemes should be encouraged to consolidate their Trust Deeds and rules at least every five years.

139. Certain basic information should be given to each employee before joining the scheme.

140. All active members and pensioners should automatically receive an annual statement.

144. Annual reports and accounts should be lodged with the pensions Registry within seven months of the scheme year end. The report and accounts should be written in plain English and the accounts signed by two trustees.

145. The actuarial valuation should be available to members within twenty-one months of the valuation date or three months of receipt from the actuary whichever is earlier.

Dispute resolution.

148. All, except small schemes, shall be required to establish a formal internal disputes procedure.

149. The Occupational Pensions Advisory Service (OPAS) should receive sufficient funding to employ paid conciliation officers.

150. The Pensions Ombudsman should not be replaced by a Tribunal but his jurisdiction should be extended.

151. The Pensions Ombudsman should be given enforcement powers.

Assignment and loss of pension rights.

159. Pension rights should be made inalienable generally, not just to obtain tax relief.

161. Scheme members should continue to be barred from instructing trustees concerning the payment of death benefits.

165. Provisions which allow pension rights to be forfeited for misconduct should be made illegal.

167. All benefits, not just GMPs, should be given immunity from creditors.

168. Forfeiture of dependants' pensions should not be allowed by reason of remarriage or cohabitation.

Ill health pensions.

170. There should be no overall rules for determining ill-health benefits.

171. Several areas are suggested where the drafting of scheme rules could be improved.

In relation to pension rights on divorce further work is recommended on the basis of the PMI Working Group on this subject.

In terms of Inland Revenue and Social Security no view was taken on fiscal policy or taxation matters but simplification was highlighted as an important aim. Disparities between social security and taxation requirements should be solved as soon as possible.

The Pensions Act and the regulator.

193. The Pensions Act should lay down a statutory framework for occupational schemes.

194. The Act should be confined to laying down principles and rules and kept separate from tax legislation or social security law.

201. Certain breaches of statutory duty should become criminal offences.

203. The Act should be supplemented by statutory and non-statutory measures including codes of practice.

209. The regulator should replace the Occupational Pensions Board.

217. The Financial Services Act regulators should continue to control investment business.

The Government welcomed the Report but clearly indicated that no legislation could be fitted in for the next two years. It seems doubtful that the sort of Bill required to deal with these recommendations and the questions raised by the European Court judgments would be introduced ahead of an election. The NAPF has recommended that the proposals be incorporated in codes of practice rather than codified by legislation.

Chapter 14

Current issues

A book like this would be incomplete without a chapter dealing with current issues, matters of concern for all pension scheme members, not specifically related to their particular scheme.

1. Overseas investment

The argument about the investment of money overseas can be emotional. The fact is that if the UK had not looked outward, it would have remained a small agricultural community. Without trade overseas, these islands would support probably no more than one-tenth of the present population. Nor can we expect to trade overseas without investing overseas.

From 1939 to 1979 there was exchange control which made overseas investment more difficult, more expensive and more risky. Naturally, when those controls were relaxed pension funds sought to take advantage of profitable situations abroad. Trustees would not invest abroad more than a balanced proportion, possibly between 10% and 20% of the money available, and they would not invest abroad at all unless they saw the prospect of a better return than that obtainable in the UK. This higher return is necessary to compensate for the additional currency risk.

From the national viewpoint, the outflow of capital will be matched by an inflow of income in the shape of interest and dividends. These inflows form part of the invisible exports which contribute so much to Britain's balance of payments. As to the argument that investing abroad denies the use of that capital to home industry, it must be remembered that the Wilson Committee in the mid 1970s found no evidence of this, and even if such a position arose it would mean that the prospects or the security of that investment were quite a long way short of the alternative investment abroad.

It must also be remembered that even where there has been a big inflow of capital, where new industries have been started up and existing ones given cash injections, the outcome has not always been very good. I am speaking here of Ireland, where there was strict exchange control, foreign firms then poured in to take advantage of tax incentives and yet inflation become higher than in the UK; the value of the Irish pound, equal to the pound sterling in 1979, was worth only 75p three years later and the unemployment level was even higher than in the UK. It was another ten years before the Irish economy stabilised.

2. Take-overs and mergers

The amount of money invested in a pension fund will vary not only according to the number of members and pensioners but also depending on what assumptions are made.

Let us suppose that Company A has 2,000 employees of varying ages who enjoy the benefits of a pension scheme which has been in existence for twenty years and offers a member's pension of one-sixtieth of pay (less an allowance for the State flat rate benefit); half widow's pension on death; and a lump sum equal to one year's pay where death occurs in service. There is a members' contribution of 5% pay. The actuary has assumed investment earnings of 8% per annum and that employees' earnings increase by 7% per annum.

Company B has two divisions, X and Y, each with 1,000 employees; its scheme has been running for ten years and it is similar to that of Company A except that members pay a 6% contribution, the lump sum death benefit is twice salary and pensions in payment are escalated each year by 3%.

Company A makes an offer to purchase the Y Division of Company B. What should happen to the pension scheme of Company B so that:

- the members of the pension scheme of Company A are not adversely affected by being joined by a large number of employees whose pension liabilities are not matched by assets;
- Company A does not have to meet such obligations in addition to the purchase price (which we must assume was itself a fair one);
- the remaining employees in the pension scheme of Company B do not see their scheme weakened (or strengthened);
- Company B does not have a reduced pension liability, beyond that appropriate to losing responsibility for the employees of Y Division?

It will be necessary to complete a full actuarial valuation of the pension scheme of Company B, using the same assumptions as have been used in previous valuations and dividing the fund according to the shares appropriate to Division X and Division Y. The Division Y share, being attributable to the Division Y employees, can be held as a separate scheme for those employees, with contributions continuing to be made as before. This may be a suitable arrangement if the division is to be run as a separate business, or the share of the scheme assets is insufficient to meet the liabilities.

If, however, the business is to be integrated, how will this be reflected in the pension arrangements? Clearly, in respect of the pensionable service to date there will be accrued benefits and these will be supported, adequately or otherwise, by the share of the scheme assets. The benefits will either be met, to the extent to which the assets will allow, or Company B will have agreed to make good the deficiency or Company A will do so. In no circumstances should the trustees of the pension scheme of Company A take on the benefit liabilities without matching assets because, in the last analysis, the existing members of the pension scheme of Company A would see their benefits diminished.

As to future service, the normal plan would be for Company A to offer membership of its own pension scheme on standard terms although, even then, if, for example, the average age of the incoming members was higher than that of existing members, the future contribution rate might have to be increased.

The detailed circumstances are so important that to generalise on this subject would be dangerous. I hope that I have 'run up enough flags' to point out the areas of difficulty.

Several important principles have been established in the area by the *Courage* case. Courage Ltd, even after it was taken over by the Imperial Group, continued to have a separate fund. This remained the case after Imperial was taken over by Hanson Trust. Hanson then sold Courage to Elders IXL, agreeing only to passing over current employees and sufficient assets to cover these members' accrued pension rights. When the case came before the court, it was held that, in the particular circumstances this could not be done. Hanson had a contingency plan which provided for the 'surplus' to go with the members, but Elders paid a higher purchase price for the company.

In general it must be preferable for these matters to be ironed out before a sale and purchase agreement is completed.

Incidentally, there was another case involving Hanson and the Imperial Fund where the court ruled that an employer did have fiduciary responsibilities to the members of its pension fund, and could not merely 'look after its own interest'. This may prove to be the more significant ruling.

3. Personal pensions

In May 1983, the Centre for Policy Studies (CPS) issued a paper calling for the radical reform of pension funds. It took as its starting point the unsatisfactory position of early leavers and developed a theory that if final pay schemes were replaced by individual personal pensions, all would be well. 'Personal pensions' thus came to mean defined contribution schemes, sometimes known as money purchase schemes. Because there is no employer to guarantee benefits under a personal pension arrangement it is impossible for it to be a final pay scheme.

Job mobility would be increased (although it was not at all clear how pension funds actually impeded the desires of employees to move), and the entrepreneurial spirit of the individual would be released to rejuvenate British industry (although how capital, which on average amounted at that time to perhaps £5,000 with an annual addition of £500 would suffice and where the management skills were to be found was glossed over).

Not too many people agreed with the CPS. The NAPF view was that the early leaver problem was already being solved (and, of course, much has happened on that front since then) and that, in any case, the CPS proposals would not reach back to solve the problems of the past. The unions feared that employers would take the opportunity to reduce costs. The Pre-Retirement Association saw that the uncertain benefits of money purchase schemes would make preparation and planning for retirement even more difficult.

The NAPF held a number of conferences that Autumn to elicit the views of the members in order to respond to the points raised by the CPS, which by that time had been adopted 'for discussion' by Government. I asked a number of questions at the London Conference, which were echoed by members everywhere:

'What does the [Government] discussion document, issued after months of discussion, seek to achieve:

- Does it want to abolish earnings-related State benefits? The proposals seemed likely to favour the opposite course. [In the event, SERPS was heavily amended in 1986 as described earlier but not to be effective until the year 2000.]
- Does it want to disband the large and efficient units of pension funds and replace them with millions of inefficient individual policies? This looked quite likely to happen. [Although several million personal pension policies are now in force, there has been no significant reduction in the number of final pay schemes although the numbers in each have dropped.]
- Does it want to replace deferred benefits on which members can plan for their retirement with a bingo-hall type package of pensions? [It is, of course, still too early to prove this point although the highly questionable selling of personal pensions has now come out in the open.]
- Does it want to try and bring into the pension net that half of the work-force not yet in? [Clearly it did, but there is little evidence to show that any large numbers of non-scheme members have become personal pension holders.]
- Does it want to enable members of approved pension schemes to do more if they wish in their own scheme? [The requirement to offer AVCs by all schemes has at least made this possible.]'

I then suggested that the Secretary of State should tell the NAPF clearly what his real objectives were and let the Association tell him how to achieve it. However, he did not do that but instead set up five committees comprising other ministers with one or two nominal outside representatives but with no representative from the opposition, from industry, from the NAPF or the unions.

In June 1985 a four volume Green paper was published. This was so widely criticised that the subsequent White Paper changed tack considerably and the Social Security Act 1986, while not ideal, was definitely workable. This is discussed next.

4. The Social Security Act 1986

The position of leavers improves with every year that passes after April 1978, because all employees earn indexed SERPS, or the equivalent contracted-out benefit, the GMP. After January 1986, defined benefits above the GMP were required to be uprated by up to 5% p.a. The Act also required that, from 1 April 1988, preservation was to become effective after only two years' membership. From 1 January 1991 all service of a leaver has to be made subject to Limited Price Indexation (LPI).

There is still no date from which pensions in course of payment must be uprated, although the Social Security Act 1990 gives power to the Secretary of State to introduce LPI at a future date. The uncertain effects of the *Barber* v *GRE* case (see paragraph 6) led the Secretary of State to state publicly that the 1990 Act provisions would be delayed. So, for the present, the only requirement for uprating pensions in course of payment commenced April 1988, when the first 3% p.a. of the GMP uprating became the responsibility of the contracted-out scheme.

The next question which the Act addressed was the cost of SERPS. Starting in the next century the target SERPS pension becomes 20% of earnings in the band between LEL and UEL after a full career. This compares with the present 25% of earnings based on earnings in a members' best twenty years. Widows will receive a pension of one half of the deceased member's pension rather than 'inheriting' an equal amount.

The effects are quite startling, altering the benefit from 1/80th of upper band earnings to less than 1/200th.

The contribution rebate for contracted-out schemes was altered to 1.8% for the employee and 3% for the employer from April 1993.

Then came some distinctly questionable requirements. An employer could not *require* an employee to join the company pension scheme. This has led to many employees opting for the cheapest course, that is, contracting back into SERPS. This is actually the opposite of what the Government professed to want. Then there was the 2% 'incentive' which the DSS added to the contribution of employees who elected to take out a personal pension. It is easy to understand the use of taxpayers' money in this way to encourage employees out of SERPS. The fact that it was available to members of final pay schemes which were already contracted-out led the NAPF to call the 2% 'a bribe'.

It has now been established that some £9 billion of public money has been spent to save, perhaps, £6 billion in the future.

Contracting-out has been made simpler, but only in its application to money purchase schemes; in fact the only requirement is to make a contribution equal to the contracting-out rebate. Personal pensions work the same way. There has been some simplification of the contracting-out procedures for final pay schemes.

But there are many other changes which support the move back to money purchase and personal pensions. The attitude of the Inland Revenue was not known until December 1986. The consultative document proposed that the only restriction would be on the amount of contribution, not on the amount of the benefit. The self-employed had always been allowed to put away up to 17.5% of their earnings in 'section 226 policies' and it was this figure which was adopted together with uplifts for older employees. The surprise here was that at age sixty-one, the employee may pay 40%. The only benefit restriction is that only one-quarter of the emerging pension may be commuted.

Another surprise in the document was a proposal to allow automatic approval for 'simplied' final pay schemes. Whereas the existing arrangements allowed a pension of one-sixtieth of final pay for each year of service equating to the Civil Service pension of one-eightieth pension plus three-eightieths final pay by way of cash, the 'simplified' scheme allows one-eightieth pension plus three one-hundredths of final pay as cash for each year of service. In addition AVCs are allowed which effectively give a greater maximum benefit than two-thirds final pay and for the purpose of determining maximum benefit the GMP may be disregarded.

The document, having effectively created seven different types of scheme:

- (a) approved participating;
- (b) approved contracted-out;
- (c) simplified participating;
- (d) simplified contracted-out;
- (e) personal participating;
- (f) personal contracted-out;
- (g) self-employed,

then ran itself into difficulties about transfers between one type and another. The ability to transfer is very important if job mobility is a key objective. For the same reasons, it was disappointing to see no reference to early retirement restrictions. The Green Paper talked of a 'decade of retirement' between age sixty and age seventy. Clearly the PSO did not agree with the idea. Finally, the range of institutions who could offer personal pensions was narrowed down to insurance companies, banks and building societies, annuities being bought from insurance companies only. This makes concepts like 'freedom of choice' seem rather empty. No one wants to see employees taken for an expensive ride, but it does seem odd that their own employers' pension funds are not regarded as capable of providing money purchase benefits at a time when the Chancellor hopes to collect much tax from the excellent investment results of these funds.

The Government promised Regulations to prevent unfair competition between pension providers and occupational pension schemes. As such schemes are required, under the 1985 Act, to quote (on members' personal statements) anticipated benefits based on current salaries, it should have been made mandatory for other potential providers to do the same. The fact that it was not, has led to the terrible situation where, perhaps, half a million personal pensions may have been sold based on a false prospectus.

5. The Social Security Act 1990

This Act has already been mentioned. It made it a requirement to grant Limited Price Indexation (LPI) to all deferred benefits of an early leaver on leaving a final pay scheme after 31 December 1990 up to that leaver's normal retirement date.

Not only is that legislation retrospective (which is inequitable since there is no requirement for an employer to have a scheme at all) but it openly discriminates once again against employers who choose to have a final pay scheme.

Another clause enables the Secretary of State to choose a date (it was originally thought it would be January 1992, but that has not proved to be the case) at which final pay schemes would have to adopt LPI, not only for deferred benefits up to NRD, but for current pensions in payment as well. Only pensions earned after the date would have to be subject to LPI except for final pay schemes with a surplus which would need to give LPI to service before the date so far as the surplus would allow. The *Barber* v *GRE* case brought such uncertainties that the Secretary of State announced a delay in choosing the date for LPI, but there has been wide speculation that, with the signing of the Protocol amending Article 119 of the Treaty of Rome in December 1991 (see below), the date might soon be announced. The fact that no mention was made in the November 1993 Budget has cast doubt on the continuing seriousness of the Government to pursue this goal.

6. The *Barber* v *Guardian Royal Exchange* case

The judgment in the case of *Barber* v *Guardian Royal Exchange*, as reported at [1993] IRLR 173, was given in the European Court of Justice on 17 May 1990. This date is destined to be the '1066' of the pensions world. It ruled that pension was 'pay' under Article 119 of the Treaty of Rome and that it was unlawful for there to be discrimination between men and women. Mr Barber had argued that, had he been a woman, his pension benefit would have been paid earlier. The Court agreed but ruled that, for the avoidance of doubt, the judgment should not be retrospective. Lawyers had a field day pronouncing their views on what that meant, and other cases were lined up in an attempt to obtain clarification.

The principal case involved a company which had gone into liquidation; the liquidator sought directions so that he was not attacked by creditors for paying too much to pensioners, or attacked by pensioners for paying too much to creditors. Once again, the judgment does not apply to money purchase schemes and for this reason alone, a 'bad' clarification could lead to a rush by employers to change their schemes away from final pay.

However, at the Maastricht 'summit' meeting in December 1991, a Protocol was agreed, which amends Article 119 so that 'pension' would not be considered as pay prior to 17 May 1990. This clarified the situation except that cases brought between May 1990 and December 1991 are proceeding.

7. The EC Directive on equal treatment for men and women

This is a typically well-intentioned effort which is likely to have quite the opposite effects from those contemplated. It requires that both contributions and benefits be equal for men and women, in spite of the fact that women live longer and retire earlier.

Most UK schemes require men and women to make an equal contribution and provide for equal benefits related to service and pay. The employer, effectively, pays a higher contribution in respect of women.

The only way to fulfil the EC conditions would be to construct average mortality or unisex mortality tables. The effect would be:

(a) to give women lower commutation cash and men more;

(b) to make transfers between pension funds subject to vicarious changes in value due to the differences in the relative numbers of men and women employed by each of the companies concerned; and

(c) to require women to forego more of their own pension in order to provide a pension or additional pension for their prospective widowers or other dependants, and men to forego less.

France, Germany and Italy do not have funded schemes, and would not be unduly affected by the Directive. However, a European Court Ruling in December 1993 in the case of Hugh Steeper, rejected the concept of unisex life tables.

Just before Christmas 1991 the Government issued a discussion document *Options for Equality in State Pension Age*. It sought views by 30 June 1992. The document was well produced and laid out the costs, advantages and disadvantages of adopting age sixty or sixty-three or sixty-five as well as discussing the concept of the decade of retirement. We had to wait until the November 1993 Budget before the Government announced its proposal to equalise state pension ages at sixty-five, the process to be complete in twenty-seven years time. Clearly this 'non decision' will be challenged.

The overwhelming majority of people over age sixty are not in paid employment and there is no real likelihood that this position will change. In any case most people want to retire at age sixty and the cost is manageable. Thus, the Government's projected figures become highly questionable.

8. The Lord Chancellor's Office consultative document on divorce and occupational pension schemes

This document, issued in July 1985, catalogued all the previous attempts to find a solution to the loss of pension expectation of a member's spouse upon divorce.

It was not clear from the paper whether its proposals dealt with widows' pensions as of right or whether it sought to embrace discretionary pensions as well. Nor did it consider State widows' pensions, which should, logically, follow the same route.

It proposed that, at the time of divorce, the court would determine whether or not it would be possible for a party to divorce proceedings to claim against the widow's pension. Then, on the member's death, the court would rule how the widow's pension would be divided. The trustees and the employer would have no part to play, and a member's wishes would have no effect. It is one of the most insensitive and impractical papers on pensions that I have read, and there are quite a few about.

The solution to the problem seemed to be far more simple. Just as member's pensions are built up year by year, so could the widow's pension. Then if there were a divorce and the member married someone else, each of the partners would 'earn' an appropriate 'widow's' pension based on the respective number of years as the member's prospective widow. For example, Mr A is a member of the XYZ pension scheme from age twenty-five with forty years' prospective service on which he can expect to earn 40/60ths of final pensionable pay. He has been married to Jane from age twenty-four but is divorced at age thirty-five. If there is a one-half widow's pension, Jane should be credited with 10/120ths of Mr A's final pensionable pay payable upon his death in service or a similar proportion of the pension he was enjoying if he had retired. If at forty he was remarried to Mary and she remained his wife until death in service, she would be entitled to 25/120ths of his final pensionable pay or, again, a similar proportion of his pension if death occurs after retirement. The pension fund is no worse off; in fact, under most present schemes Mary would receive 40/120ths, and the likelihood is that she is younger than Jane so the fund would be better off on two scores. In these days of equality one would expect an identical treatment in respect of a female member of a pension scheme.

However, events moved on and the PMI set up a committee to give fresh consideration. The Goode Committee considered that this work should continue.

9. Member participation in running schemes

Finally, and I hope you have derived as much pleasure from reading this book as I have writing it, we come to the question of member participation in the running of the scheme. Early in 1982 the NAPF published a *Guide to Good Practice* on this matter. The principles which it states are quite short and are quoted in full below:

'*Principles*

Pension Schemes exist to provide benefits for members and their dependants. It is therefore logical and reasonable, whether the scheme is contributory or non-contributory, that members should participate in the operation of the scheme.

The NAPF does not believe that any one participative system is necessarily better than another but rather that each employer should develop the one best suited to his own situation.

The individuals to be involved in participation should be chosen by a process designed to ensure as far as possible that they are representative of employees who are members of the pension scheme. The interest of other beneficiaries, especially pensioners, should not be overlooked.

Appropriate arrangements should be set up for training these individuals in the performance of their duties and for them to communicate with the members of the pension scheme.'

It goes on to deal with *Practical Guidelines*. For example, it suggests that it is reasonable to have an equal number of employees appointed by the employing company and elected by some democratic process by the members. It states that, particularly where the employing company meets the 'balance of cost', the Chairman with a casting vote may be appointed by the employing company. It does, however, report the experience of most pension fund managers that 'trustees will normally operate by consensus and the need to vote at all will rarely arise'.

Most importantly, it suggests that all trustees should recognise that:

(a) They must carry out to the best of their ability the proper duties of trustees ensuring:
- the keeping of proper accounts
- the correct application and observance of the rules
- the safeguarding and prudent investment of the fund's assets for which they are responsible
- the provision of adequate information to all members regarding the scheme and its administration.

(b)   They must have regard to the interest of all members, beneficiaries and contingent beneficiaries of the scheme and not just those of any particular group of members.

(c)   It is no part of their roles as trustees to initiate or negotiate with the employer changes in the provisions of the scheme.

It cannot be over-stressed that suitable training is extremely important. The Guide is only five pages long but it is well worth reading.

10. The Maxwell affair

I waited a long time before releasing this manuscript because of the unfinished business of *Barber* and the date under the Social Security Act 1990 requiring LPI for those in receipt of pensions. I had little idea of yet another matter which would burst upon the scene. I refer to the Robert Maxwell affair. Although it is not, strictly speaking, a pension matter, it draws attention to the need for trustees to be vigilant in their duties. I am sure there will be more legislation in an attempt to curb the activities of another Maxwell, most of which will only lay further burdens on the other 99.999% of pension administrators. The really important change which could be made would be to require an independent trustee for each approved pension scheme. Personally, as a potential independent trustee, I should be delighted to see such a requirement, but to find a sufficient number of suitable people would be extremely difficult.

There are other sensible changes which could be ordered:

●   that companies could not be the trustees of their own pension schemes;

●   that a subsidiary of the employing company could not be appointed investment manager;

●   that the trustees should appoint auditors different from those of the employing company; and

●   that, on a take-over, a different firm of actuaries should be appointed by the trustees.

I wish you all a long and happy retirement.

Appendix 1

Typical draft interim trust deed

(see Chapter 3)

THIS INTERIM TRUST DEED is made the .... day of ....
199... BETWEEN [Company] whose registered office is at [address] ('the
Principal Employer') of the one part and [names and addresses of trustees] ('the
Trustees') of the other part.

WHEREAS
(1) The Principal Employer has resolved to establish under irrevocable trusts the
    [name of Scheme] ('the Scheme') for providing relevant benefits as defined in
    Section 612(1) of the Income and Corporation Taxes Act 1988 ('the 1988
    Act') for such of its employees as are or become eligible to participate in
    accordance with the provisions governing the Scheme to be set out in a
    definitive trust deed ('the Definitive Trust Deed') and in the rules ('the Rules')
    to be made under the provisions thereof.
(2) It is intended that the Scheme shall be Contracted-Out under the terms of the
    Social Security Pensions Act 1975 (as amended) ('the 1975 Act') and
    regulations made under that Act.
(3) The Principal Employer has resolved to appoint the Trustees to act as the
    trustees of the Scheme.

NOW THIS DEED WITNESSETH and it is agreed and declared as follows:
1. The Principal Employer hereby establishes the Scheme to commence with
   effect from [date] and constitutes the Fund under irrevocable trusts to be
   administered in accordance with the provisions of this Deed the Definitive
   Deed and the Rules as from time to time amended.
2. The Principal Employer hereby appoints the Trustees to be the trustees of the
   Scheme.
3. The Principal Employer and the Trustees hereby undertake to execute a
   Definitive Deed not later than 24 months from the date of this Deed which
   Definitive Deed together with the Rules shall be prepared in such a way:-
   (a) that the Scheme is capable of approval by the Board of Inland Revenue
       and of treatment as an exempt approved scheme under Chapter 1 of Part
       XIV of the 1988 Act or any statutory modification or re-enactment of
       the 1988 Act for the time being in force
   (b) that the benefits under the Scheme shall be preserved in accordance with
       the requirements of Section 63 of the Social Security Act 1973 (as
       amended) and Part 1 of Schedule 16 to that Act (as amended) and
       regulations under that Act
   (c) that the Scheme shall be operated in conformikty with the requirements
       of equal access as required by Sections 53 to 56 of the 1975 Act
   (d) that membership of the Scheme may be treated as Contracted-Out
       Employment under the terms of the 1975 Act (as amended) and
       regulations made under that Act.

4. Until the execution of the Definitive Deed the Principal Employer shall pay such contributions as the Trustees acting on the advice of an Actuary (being a Fellow of the Institute of Actuaries or a Fellow of the Faculty of Actuaries in Scotland) may from time to time decide PROVIDED THAT no such contributions shall be paid as would prejudice the approval of the Scheme by the Board of Inland Revenue under Chapter 1 of Part XIV of the 1988 Act.

5. The power of appointing new or additional trustees of the Scheme and the power of removing one or more of the trustees shall be vested in the Principal Employer and shall be exercised by deed.

6. The Trustees shall be entitled to all indemnities conferred on trustees by law and none of the Trustees or a director employee or member of a body corporate being one of the Trustees for the time being shall be liable for any acts or omissions not due to their or his own wilful neglect or default and the Principal Employer shall keep the Trustees indemnified against the exercise of all the trustees' powers and the application of the trustees' discretion.

7. All costs charges and expenses whatever incurred in or about the establishment administration and management of the Scheme (other than the cost of the acquisition or disposal of investments which shall be borne by the Fund) shall be paid by the Principal Employer.

IN WITNESS whereof the Principal Employer has caused its Common Seal to be hereunto affixed and the Trustees have executed this Deed the day and year first before written.

Appendix 2

Typical draft deed of extension

(see Chapter 3)

THIS DEED OF EXTENSION is made the .... day of .... 199...
BETWEEN [Company] whose registered office is at [address] ('the Employer') of
the one part and [name and address of the trustees] ('the Trustees') of the other
part.

WHEREAS
(1) This Deed is supplemental to (inter alia) an Interim Trust Deed dated [date]
    ('the Interim Trust Deed') constituting the Scheme therein described ('the
    Scheme').
(2) The Trustees are the present trustees of the Scheme.
(3) By virtue of the Interim Trust Deed the Employer undertook with the
    Trustees that it would within [period] execute a Definitive Trust Deed
    adopting Rules to govern the Scheme.
(4) Such Definitive Trust Deed not having been executed within the said period
    of [period] the Trustees have agreed to enter into this Deed to extend the time
    period therefor.

NOW THIS DEED WITNESSETH and it is HEREBY AGREED AND
DECLARED that the period of [period] referred to in the Interim Trust Deed
shall be and is hereby extended by a further [period] to [date].

IN WITNESS whereof the Employer has caused its Common Seal to be hereunto
affixed and the Trustees have executed this Deed the day and year first before
written.

Appendix 3

Typical draft deed of appointment

(see Chapter 3)

THIS DEED OF APPOINTMENT is made the .... day of ....
199... BETWEEN [Company] whose registered office is at [address] ('the
Principal Employer') of the first part [names and addresses of continuing trustees]
('the Continuing Trustees') of the second part and [name and address of new
trustee] ('the New Trustee') of the third part.

WHEREAS
(1) This Deed is supplemental to (inter alia) a Trust Deed dated [date] ('the Trust
    Deed') the terms and conditions of which govern the [name of scheme] ('the
    Scheme').
(2) [name of retiring trustee] ('the Retiring Trustee') and the Continuing
    Trustees are the present trustees of the Scheme.
(3) The Principal Employer is desirous of appointing the New Trustee in place of
    the Retiring Trustee.

NOW THIS DEED WITNESSETH that with effect from the date hereof the
Principal Employer in exercise of the power conferred upon it by the Trust Deed
and of every and any other power it enabling HEREBY APPOINTS the New
Trustee to be a trustee of the Scheme to act jointly with the Continuing Trustees
for the purposes of the trusts thereof in place of the Retiring Trustee who is
discharged from the said trusts.

IN WITNESS whereof the Principal Employer has caused its Common Seal to be
hereunto affixed and the Continuing Trustees and the New Trustee have executed
this Deed the day and year first before written.

Appendix 4

Example expression of wish letter

(see Chapters 3 and 8)

DEATH BENEFITS NOMINATION FORM OR 'WISH LETTER'

TO: THE XYZ PENSION FUND TRUSTEES
FROM: (member's full name)

I have completed this form to help you decide how to apply the benefits which arise in respect of me.
* I have/have not made a Will, but I understand that benefits arising under the pension scheme do not fall to be dealt with by me in such a document.
I understand that you have absolute discretion and that you may consider a range of possible beneficiaries.
I understand that this form will be kept sealed until I request you to return it to me or until the benefit arises. Accordingly, I realise that it is my responsibility to amend my wishes if circumstances change.
I set out briefly the reasons for expressing my wishes.
I should like you to consider applying the benefits as follows:

	Name	Address	Relationship (if any)	Share of Benefit (if more than one name given)
1.	....	....	....	....
2.	....	....	....	....
3.	....	....	....	....

My reasons are as follows:

Signed: .... Date: ....
* Please delete 'have' or 'have not'

Appendix 5A

Example benefit statement (final pay scheme)

(see Chapter 3)

To: [*name of member in full*] N.I. Number: [*or other reference*]
From: The Chairman/Secretary to the Trustees of the XYZ Pension Scheme

Based upon the following data:
(a) your date of birth being [*date*];
(b) your membership dating from [*date*];
(c) your normal retirement date [*date*] at age [*age*];
(d) your expected period of pensionable service [*years and months*];
(e) your current pensionable earnings of £ ...... per annum,
and the following factors:-
(f) your final pensionable earnings are the same as your current pensionable earnings;
(g) the pension factor remains [1/720th] of final pensionable earnings for each complete month of pensionable service;
(h) [*where appropriate*] the deductor from actual pay remains [equal to the State flat rate benefit for a single person, currently (£57 a week)];
then your personal pension [guaranteed to be paid for five years] will be £ ......
per annum [paid in advance on 1st of each month].
Under current legislation you would be entitled to exchange part of that pension for a tax free lump sum.
Your pension will be increased by [5% per annum or the percentage increase in the Retail Prices Index if lower].

If you die in service leaving [a spouse or other dependant] a pension of [one-half] the amount of your anticipated pension will be paid to [that spouse or other dependant]. [The spouse's pension will be payable for life/the dependant's pension will be payable on terms set out by the Trustees.]

The Trustees will also have discretion to pay to a range of possible beneficiaries a sum equal to [three times] your then current pay. In this connection you are invited to complete a nomination form to assist the Trustees in reaching their decision.

If you die in retirement leaving [a spouse or other dependant] a pension of [one-half] the amount of your pension (increased to take account of any lump sum you received in exchange for part of your original entitlement) will be paid to [that spouse or other dependant]. [The spouse's pension will be payable for life/the dependant's pension will be payable on terms set out by the Trustees.]

If you leave the service of the company before becoming entitled to a pension there are a number of options available to you which will be advised to you at that time.

Appendix 5B

Example benefit statement (money purchase scheme)

(see Chapter 3)

To: [*name of member in full*] N.I. Number: [*or other reference*]
From: The Chairman/Secretary to the Trustees of the XYZ Pension Scheme.

Your personal account as at [6th April 1993] stood at £ . . . .
In the year to [5th April 1994] there has been added:

* your contributions   £ . . . .
* the company contributions   £ . . . .
* your share of the fund's:
  - investment earnings   £ . . . .
  - capital appreciation (depreciation)   £ . . . .

So that your personal account as
at [5th April 1994] stands at   £ . . . .
Based on the following data:-

(a) your date of birth being [*date*];
(b) your normal retirement date being [*date*] at age [*age*];
(c) your contributions and those of the company remaining at the same levels as the past year, shown above;
(d) your share of the fund growing at an annual rate of [8%];
(e) the rate at which your personal account could be converted to pension at your normal retirement date being [£11] per £1 per annum pension;

then your personal pension would be £ . . . . per annum [paid in arrears on the last day of each month].
The factor shown at (e) above can be varied to include:

(i) a five year guarantee;
(ii) a spouse's/dependant's pension on your death;
(iii) annual increases during payment.

If you die in service the then value of your personal account will be used to buy a pension for [your spouse/dependant].
[The company makes additional payments to secure a death in service lump sum in respect of you equal to [twice] your annual pay and the Trustees have discretion to pay that sum to a range of beneficiaries.
In this connection you are invited to complete a nomination form to assist the Trustees in reaching their decision.]

If you leave the service of the company before becoming entitled to a pension there are a number of options available to you which will be advised to you at that time.

119

Appendix 6

List of memoranda extant at July 1991

Extracted from Joint Office Memorandum No.106 — Relocation of PSO and OPB — July 1991
(note: for SFO now read PSO)

No.	Issued by	Title
No.13	SFO	Value of pensions with entitlement to post-retirement increases.
No.23	OPB	Assistance to occupational pension schemes in modification or winding up.
No.25	SFO	Part I Final remuneration for calculation of maximum benefits.
		Part II 20% directors — normal retirement age.
No.27	SFO	Transfer of pension rights between the United Kingdom and the Republic of Ireland and arrangements for the tax treatment of retirement benefit schemes approved by the Commissioners of Inland Revenue in the UK and by the Revenue Commissioners in the Republic of Ireland.
No.32	OPB	Equal access to occupational pension schemes for men and women.
No.37	SFO	Effect on tax approval of future amendments to 'Old Code' occupational pension schemes.
No.46	SFO	Pensions terminating at State pensionable age.
No.50	OPB	Interim documentation (paragraphs 20 and 21 only).
No.54	SFO	Part I Salary sacrifices.
		Part II Refunds of employee's contributions — the £5,000 earnings limit.
		Part III Contracted-out schemes — commutation.
No.58	SFO	Small Self-Administered Schemes.
No.59	SFO	20% directors — Death benefits.
No.60	SFO	Inland Revenue treatment of 'Old Code' schemes after 5 April 1980.
No.63	SFO	Occupational pension schemes: Notes on approval under the Finance Act 1970 as amended by the Finance Act 1971 — IR 12 (May 1979), replacing IR 12 (October 1974).
No.64	SFO	Refunds of employees' contributions — the £5,000 earnings limit.
No.65	SFO	Part I Administrator.
		Part II Pensioners resident abroad.
No.66	OPB	Contracting-out: elections and related procedures.
No.74	OPB	Contracting-out: occupational pension schemes which cease to be contracted-out.
No.75	OPB	Application of the preservation, equal access and

No.	Issued by	Title
		contracting-out requirements to schemes with an overseas element: transfer of benefit rights to overseas schemes.
No.76	OPB	Contracting-out: supervision of scheme resources — revised actuarial certificates and other matters.
No.77	OPB	Contracting-out: salary related schemes — rule requirements.
No.78	OPB	Preservation, revaluation and transfer values (cash equivalents).
No.79	SFO	Funding of insured schemes — earmarked policies.
No.80	SFO	Change of employment.
No.81	SFO	Monetary limits: Part I Changes of Inland Revenue practice: Retained benefits etc. Part II Amendments to practice notes and joint office memoranda.
No.5 (Amending) SFO		Part I Changes in SFO practice.
No.6 (Amending) SFO		Part III Changes in SFO practice.
No.82	SFO	New rules for dealing with pension fund surpluses.
No.84	OPB	Disclosure of information by occupational pension schemes.
No.85	SFO	Buying-out: Inland Revenue requirements and associated matters.
No.86	SFO	Pension scheme surpluses.
No.87	SFO	Tax reform package for pensions: legislative changes and transitional arrangements.
No.88	SFO	Schedule 3 Finance (No 2) Act 1987 and changes in Inland Revenue Practice.
No.89	SFO	Free-Standing Additional Voluntary Contributions schemes.
No.90	SFO	Part I Applications for Inland Revenue approval. Part II Notification of Inland Revenue approval. Part III Salary sacrifices.
No.91	SFO	Finance (No 2) Act 1987 and changes in Inland Revenue practice.
No.92	OPB	Personal pension schemes: social security requirements for all schemes and contracting-out requirements for appropriate schemes.
No.93	OPB	Money purchase contracting-out: scheme rule requirements.
No.94	SFO	Occupational pension schemes: approval under FA 1970: simplified schemes.
No.95	SFO	Personal pension schemes and retirement annuity contracts.
No.96	SFO	Part I Contracted-out money purchase schemes — SFO aspects. Part II Contracted-out money purchase schemes — simplified schemes. Part III Refunds of contributions. Part IV Final remuneration. Part V Transfers.

No.	Issued by	Title
No.97	SFO	Part I General note. Part II Amendments to IR 76 (Guidance notes on personal pensions). Part III Transfers to personal pensions schemes from occupational schemes and deferred annuity contracts. Part IV Amendments to IR 12 (1979) FSAVC supplement. Part V Minimum contribution only personal pension schemes.
No.98	SFO	Part I Simplified defined contribution schemes. Part II Member's contributions. Part III Schemes for professional footballers.
No.99	SFO	Part I Introduction. Part II The proposals affecting occupational schemes and AVC schemes. Part III Effect on procedures. Part IV Personal pension schemes. Part V Effect on PPS procedures.
No.100	SFO	Part I Introduction. Part II Schedules 6 and 7 Finance Act 1989. Part III Amendments to IR 12 (1979) — The Practice Notes. Part IV Effect on schemes and procedures. Part V Simplified schemes. Part VI Free-Standing Additional Voluntary Contribution schemes. Part VII Other practice changes. Part VIII Pension scheme surpluses. Part IX Personal pension schemes. Part X Superannuation Funds Office fax number.
No.101	SFO	Personal Pension Schemes. Part I Investment of members' contributions. Part II Use of scheme funds.
No.102	SFO	Compliance audit of retirement benefit schemes.
No.103	OPB	Operation of the Register and collection of the Levy.
No.104	SFO	Part I Inter regime transfers. Part II Schemes approved under Chapter I Part XIV ICTA: Miscellaneous. Part III Minor amendments to IR 12 (1979) The Practice Notes.
No.105	SFO	Applications for Inland Revenue Approval: documentation certificates.
No.106	SFO & OPB	Relocation of SFO and OPB.

Memoranda issued after July 1991 are available respectively from the PSO ((081) 398 4242) or the OPB ((091) 225 6414/6417).

Appendix 7

Draft death benefit trustees' questionnaire

(see Chapter 8)

QUESTIONNAIRE TO ASSIST TRUSTEES IN EXERCISING
DISCRETION OVER PAYMENT OF DEATH BENEFITS

TO: XYZ PERSONNEL OFFICE
FROM: XYZ PENSION FUND TRUSTEES

A. Please complete as fully as possible and as soon as practical this Questionnaire (and return to Pensions Office) in respect of:
(Member's name:)

N.I. number: .... Date of death: ....

B. Member's address:
Original of Death Certificate dated .... enclosed/forwarded to you.

Earnings since 6th April last: £ ....
It appears that the following person was accepting responsibility for funeral expenses:
Name: .... Relationship or other status: ....

C. To be completed following detailed interview. Please despatch Part B if there is to be delay of more than 7 days.
The member left the following dependants:-

Name	Relationship (if any)	Date of birth	Remarks
1.	....	....	....
2.	....	....	....
3.	....	....	....
4.	....	....	....

The member lived in:
(i)   own property (subject to £ .... mortgage protected/not protected by life insurance), or,
(ii) rented accommodation, or,
(iii) other (*give details*):

The member left a Will (*give details*):
Or, letters of administration are being taken out by: ....

Spouse's birth [and marriage] certificate[s] enclosed.
Children's/other dependants' birth certificates enclosed.

Signed: .... Position: .... Date: ....

(Please write separately any additional comments or information)

Appendix 8

Draft death benefit trustees'/committee recommendation

(see Chapter 8)

RECOMMENDATION TO TRUSTEES IN EXERCISING
DISCRETION OVER PAYMENT OF DEATH BENEFITS

TO: THE TRUSTEES OF THE XYZ PENSION SCHEME
FROM: THE SECRETARY TO THE TRUSTEES

A. IT IS RECOMMENDED that the benefits in respect of [*name in full*] be paid as follows, based on the information set out below:

Death grant £ [*full amount*] to be paid to:
a. [*name & relationship*] £ [*amount*]
b. [*if more than one*] [*name & relationship*] £ [*amount*]
c. [*name & relationship*] £ [*amount*]
Spouse's/dependant's pension(s) to be paid to:
(i) [*name & relationship*] £ [*amount*] per annum
(ii) [*if more than one*] [*name & relationship*] £ [*amount*] per annum
(iii) [*name & relationship*] £ [*amount*] per annum
(Note if any pensions stop, for example, at age 18.)

B. The member [*name in full*] whose date of birth was [*date*] and who joined the scheme [*date*] died on [*date*] from [*causes on death certificate*]. The member's pension at normal retirement date was anticipated to be £ [*amount*] per annum. The member left dependants/relations as follows:

Name	Relationship (if any)	Date of birth	Remarks
1.	....	....	....
2.	....	....	....
3.	....	....	....
4.	....	....	....

The member lived in the following type of accommodation: [*give details*]

The member left a Will/letters of administration are being taken out by: [*give name & relationship*]

Details of the terms of the Will are as follows: [*give details*]

C. Please return one copy of this recommendation stating that:
a. I agree, or,
b. I require further information regarding the matters noted below, or,
c. I do not agree, please call a meeting to discuss.

Signed: .... Date: ....

124

Appendix 9

Typical investment policy framework letter

(see Chapter 10)

'Dear Sirs,

This letter sets out the terms agreed to be effective [*date*].

1. You are responsible (subject to such further agreements as may be reached from time to time) for the investment of:
    (a) the XYZ Pension Fund: 'A' Portfolio of securities and cash as at present constituted; together with
    (b) net income arising from your portfolio; and
    (c) new money allocated to your portfolio as advised from time to time.
2. The basis will be:
    (a) Equities (including Convertibles) —
         The total value will not exceed [70%] of the value of the Fund and the overseas content will not exceed [25%] of the Fund.
    (b) Fixed Interest —
         No holding to exceed an amount which is reasonably marketable or to be of such an amount that a sale would unduly depress the price.
    (c) Cash —
         [Cash not immediately used for stock exchange investment will be invested in short-term deposits; the depository selected will be:
         (i) one of those included on a list agreed by all the Fund's advisers and approved by the Trustees;
         (ii) subject to restrictions recommended by your house and approved by the Trustees as to the maximum amount to be deposited with any depository; both the list and the restrictions will be subject to amendment following the recommendations of your House and approval of the Trustees from time to time.]
    (d) Special Situations —
         [e.g. the purchase of shares in an unquoted company and in-house investment(s) to be exploited subject to prior agreement between your House and the Trustees.]
    (e) Property —
         The total value will not exceed [15%] of the value of the Fund and no single property will exceed [2%] of the value of the Fund.
    (f) Self-investment —
         No more than 5% is permitted to be invested in any form of security where the employing company is involved.
3. You will include in the regular reports to the Trustees details of transactions during the previous quarter. In addition, you will report in writing at the time of first purchase or each first sale of each new security stating briefly your reasons. You will also supply on request in writing, your reasons for effecting any particular transaction.

125

    e portfolio performance will be measured quarterly:
    (a) by the combined income, net profits or losses and capital appreciation or depreciation achieved;
   (b) against a mixed index based on the actual distribution of total stock exchange portfolio investments, or on such other basis or against such other indices as may be agreed;
   (c) participation in the [WM] measurement service will be required.
5. The portfolio will be revalued and reviewed at least annually.
6. Representations to have this investment policy framework varied will be considered by the Trustees.
7. The annual fee [payable quarterly in arrears calculated on a pro rata time basis] will be based on the following scale:

Amount under management (£M)   *Fee scale (%)*

....
....
....

The portfolio valuation will be reduced by the value of any in-house investments.'

Bibliography

Most of the more general books published in the last few years have become out of date because of the tremendous amount of legislation which has been enacted. Specialist works have been affected more so. Most public libraries now keep books on pensions, although the date of publication needs to be watched carefully.
The PMI and NAPF publications are constantly updated, and lists follow.

Publications of The Pensions Management Institute, PMI House, 4–10 Artillery Lane, London E1 7LS, telephone (071) 247 1452
Getting your A.P.M.I., £2.00
The Impact of Inflation on Pension Funds (revised 1984), £3.00
Pensions and Divorce (1991), £21.00
PMI Year Book (1993), £60.00
Pensions Terminology (Joint PMI/PRAG Publication) (1992), £7.00
PMI Tuition Manuals, (1993–1994), £40.00 per subject
   1 — Introduction to Pension Schemes and Social Security
   2 — Law
   3 — Taxation
   4 — Scheme Design
   5 — Scheme Constitution and Documentation
   6 — Scheme Administration and Financing
   7 — Scheme Investment
   8 — Remuneration and Other Benefits
   9 — Communication and Management

Publications of The National Association of Pension Funds, 12–18 Grosvenor Gardens, London SW1W 0DH, telephone (071) 730 0585

Annual Publications		Members £	Non-Members £
NAPF Year Book 1994		27.50	50.00
Survey of Occupational Pension Schemes 1992		48.00	96.00
Survey of Occupational Pension Schemes 1991		48.00	96.00
NAPF Pensions Legislation Service		171.00	190.00
Miscellaneous			
The Role of the Pension Fund Trustee	1–5 copies	15.95	15.95
by John Conliffe	6 or more	13.25	15.95

Bibliography

		Members £	Non-Members £
Investment			
Creative Tension?		5.00	10.00
Committee of Enquiry Report into		10.00	40.00
Investment Performance Measurement			
Visibility of Investment Management Fees		10.00	20.00
A Working Group Report			
Notes on Pensions Series			
No.12 — Accounting for Overseas		3.00	4.00
Investments by UK Pension Funds			
No.13 — Data Protection Act 1984		1.85	2.80
No.17 — Pension Scheme Annual Reports		3.00	4.00
No.18 — Accounting for Insurance		3.00	4.00
Policies in Pension Schemes			
No.20 — Investment Management—	1 – 5 copies	3.00	4.00
A Guide for Trustees	6 or more	2.50	3.50
No.21 — Trust Deed and Rules Checklist	1 – 5 copies	3.00	4.00
	6 or more	2.50	3.50
Leaflets (discounts available for bulk purchases)			
Early Leaver's Guide	10 copies	5.00	7.50
New Employee's Leaflet			
(Specify Final Salary or Money Purchase version)	20 copies	5.00	7.50

Also available free to Members and Non-Members
Pension Fund Investment Performance Code; Share Scheme Guidelines; The Pre-Emption Principle; The Role and Duties of Directors; Responsibilities of Institutional Shareholders in the UK; Management Buy-Outs; The Annual Report of the NAPF's Investment Committee; Guide to Pensions Organisations; Checklist for Pension Fund Trustees; Checklist on Uptake of Scheme Membership; and Checklist on Visibility of Investment Management Fees.

Index

Index